George M. Fairchild

Rod and Canoe

Rifle and Snowshoe in Quebec's Adirondacks

George M. Fairchild

Rod and Canoe
Rifle and Snowshoe in Quebec's Adirondacks

ISBN/EAN: 9783337258610

Printed in Europe, USA, Canada, Australia, Japan

Cover: Foto ©Andreas Hilbeck / pixelio.de

More available books at **www.hansebooks.com**

ROD and CANOE,

RIFLE and SNOWSHOE

—— IN ——

Quebec's Adirondacks

BY

G. M. FAIRCHILD, Jr.,

EDITOR OF CANADIAN LEAVES, ETC.

QUEBEC:
PRINTED BY FRANK CARREL
DAILY TELEGRAPH Office.

1896

REGISTERED in the Office of the Minister of Agriculture in conformity with the law passed by the Parliament of Canada, in the year 1893, by the author, G. M. Fairchild, Jr.

To

THE HON. JOHN SHARPLES, QUEBEC, CANADA,

AND

ROBERT BLEAKIE, ESQ., BOSTON, MASS., U. S.

with the affectionate regards of the Author.

"Ravenscliffe,"
    Cap Rouge, Quebec,

May 5th, 1896.

PREFATORY NOTE.

In the following pages I have embodied, in a somewhat altered form to suit the scope of the present work, one or two contributions of my own to various publications in the United States, notably that sportsman's old favorite "The Forest and Stream."

I am conscious of the many shortcomings in my attempt to exploit Quebec's lake regions, but should it inspire some one to undertake a fuller and more complete work, I shall be among the first to rejoice and to extend a right hearty welcome to the new comer.

TABLE OF CONTENTS.

Chap.   I.—Quebec's Adirondacks.

"   II.—Quebec—Lake St. Charles.

"   III.—Lake Beauport.

"   IV.—The Jacques Cartier River.

"   V.—Lake St. Joseph.

"   VI.—In the Kingdom of the Tourilli Club.

"   VII.—Lakes Tantari and Belle Truite.

"   VIII.—The Laurentides National Park.

"   IX.—Lake Edward.

"   X.—Ouananiche Fishing—Lake St. John.

"   XI.—Angling Notes.

"   XII.—Caribou Hunting.

"   XIII.—Fishing Clubs—Game Laws.

QUEBEC OF OLD.

CHAPTER FIRST.

QUEBEC'S ADIRONDACKS.

"Laurentia ! Superb Laurentia !
 Thy mountains in the garments of the cloud ;
 Thy rivers pouring down o'er crystal leagues
 Their glassy waters to the solemn sea ;
 Thine isle-gemmed lakes ; thine old, old solitudes."

The city of Quebec is the portal to the last remaining kingdom of the angler-sportsman. The dark purple Laurentides, frowning grimly into the smiling face of the valley of the St. Lawrence and upon the rocky heights of the city of Champlain, are the outer barriers of a vast primeval wilderness whose only northern boundary is the great arctic land. In the rugged fastnesses of the mountains this modern despot sets at defiance the further progress of civilization and reigns supreme over a limitless territory. His subjects are the few scattered Indian tribes, the adventurous *coureurs de bois*, and his guides. With these forces at his command he lays tribute upon the untamed beasts of the forest, and the fishes of the lakes and rivers. No wassailing king of ancient days held higher revelry within his court, than does this wild-land ruler within the charmed circle of his little camp fire amidst the gloom of solemn forests, the roar of rushing waters. He has drank at the fountain of health, and his intoxication is that of complete freedom, of simple living in the great outdoor of nature, the excitement of the chase, the indescribable charm of angling in the rough rivers of the North land, or upon the placid bosom of forest girt lake. And it brings the glow of strength, the consciousness of power, and mental rest.

OLD PRESCOTT GATE.

The very nearness of this land of savage Nature to the old civilization within the gates of Quebec is one of the startling features which first arrests the attention of the visiting angler-sportsman, and, if he is close of observation, he will not fail to further note that it has left a certain impress upon the male population at least. They are full of the legend and lore of the bush. The charm of the life has entered into their hearts, and is a part of their being, born in them perhaps from ancestry, who fought the wilderness from love of adventure, and the gain of pelfry. It makes good fellows of them, and the camp fire glow is enlivened by the comradeship of one of these big hearted, unselfish, thorough going sportsmen.

These irregular, broken, forest covered, picturesque old Laurentides are the silent, hoary guardians of vast inland seas, lakes and lakelets, whose numbers are as the leaves of the trees. Sheltered and guarded by overhanging mountain and dense forest they have slowly unbosomed themselves to the adventurous angler, and even to-day, well within sound of the Citadel gun of Quebec, there are still hidden away numbers of little lakes that blushingly await his coming. The very great irregularity of this primitive earth's upheaval almost defies a complete exploration of its surface, but enough has been accomplished to prove the rest, and to the sportsman is left the added pleasure of new discoveries to whet his appetite, for every bit of living water contains trout; and caribou and moose seek the seclusion of these unvisited lakes on whose borders they feed and increase. Here too the beavers love to build their dams,

VIEW FROM KING'S BASTION.

and create colonies. I have discovered dozens of lakes, and lost them again, swallowed up in the great forest, but I felt no regret at this for there were always others unexpectedly turning up. Following a caribou trail one winter's day I crossed no less than five of these little mountain lakes, and they were innocent of man until then, a white man at any rate. I fished one where I camped in the snow that night and caught four or five 1 lb. fish, just enough for a hungry man's supper and breakfast.

The rivers flowing from the mountains and emptying into the river St. Lawrence or Lake St. John are the arteries of this region, through which the angler-sportsman may find his way into the heart of the land of lakes, for it is on the table land of the divide where they expand into vast bodies of water, extend in chains of unknown length, where one may canoe for days at a stretch, and fish until the arm drops helpless, and the appetite cloys with satiety. And if it is in the early autumn, when all nature seems putting forth its final notes of rejoicing, and the mountains are clad in a wealth of coloring, the rifle will alternate with the rod, and a caribou or perhaps a moose will further gladden the heart of him who seeks.

Another and important highway into this kingdom is the Quebec and Lake St. John R.R., which was constructed to bring the parishes surrounding this famous lake into communication with the greater world. For two hundred miles it was literally pushed into the wilderness; but a wilderness it will remain notwithstanding the iron-horse and band of steel, for the mightier forces of nature have proclaimed this intervening territory as only the empire of the sportsman, and the latter with sovereign authority has turned the railroad to his own purpose. The very stations on the

RETURN OF THE HUNTSMEN.

road are but the camps of individual sportsmen, or clubs which have been organized for good fellowship, trout and game. The railroad, quick to recognize the controlling force of destiny, has placed its resources at the command of this ruling power, and the road might be justly called the Quebec & Lake St. John, Anglers' and Sportsmen's R.R. You have but to board one of its outgoing or incoming trains and this fact is driven home. It is in possession of Indians, guides, sportsmen and anglers, with their impedimenta of canoes, packs, rifles and rod cases. The conversation amid dense clouds of smoke is of the bush, fishy or gamy. Mighty yarns are spun, and were the shades of Baron Munchausen to present themselves, they would be put to the blush, by these later knights of the long bow; but everything goes, as the saying has it, for the etiquette of the craft frowns upon any doubt being cast upon the credibility of one of the fraternity.

Lake St. John, the objective point of the Railroad, is but the beginning again of another sportsman's land of plenty. In the lake itself, its tributary rivers, the Grand Discharge, the ouananiche, that gamiest of the *salmo* family, makes its home. In close proximity to the best fishing grounds two famous hotels have been built for the accommodation of anglers. When tired of the luxury of the life here one can take Indian guides at Pointe Bleue and strike boldly into the wilderness to seek the mysterious Lake Mistassini.

Upon the borderland of the Laurentides dwell a

singular people, a race long settled upon the land they till, but who, amidst the progress of the last two centuries, have successfully resisted its encroachments, and to-day exhibit the strange anomaly of French customs, manners and habits of the 17th century preserved to the 19th in the new world, under a foreign government. A happier, more contented peasantry do not exist, and their virtues are manifold. They are a social, loving people, and delight to live within sound of the parish church bell. Very devout, they have an immense number of *fête* days, during which all labor is suspended to enable them to attend the mass, and the subsequent festivities. Sunday is pre-eminently the happiest day of the week. If in summer, no sooner is mass concluded than the whole parish adjourn to the greensward upon the river bank to partake of their frugal meal amid much raillery and laughter, and then the afternoon is given up to dancing and singing, courting and canoeing, and other innocent amusements.

They labor no harder than is necessary to provide for their simple wants. They are a self-contained people, and extreme indigence is rare among them. The wives and daughters spin and weave their own linen and woolen cloth wherewith they clothe themselves; their small farms yield sufficient for the family use; the maple bush the sugar and syrup; the nearest stream or lake abundance of luscious trout for fast days; the *sapin* swamp its quota of snared hares and partridges. They have little to sell, still less to purchase.

They are exceedingly courteous and polite in their intercourse with each other and toward strangers; even the little children bow and courtesy on the road when passing you. They are hospitable in the extreme, and anticipate the every wish of the traveler who seeks their door. Above all they are devoted to their native soil, *le beau* **Canada**. When the long arctic winter spreads o'er the land, and all labor is suspended, the people abandon themselves to the delights of that social intercourse of which they are so fond. Day and night the roads resound with the lively tinkling of sleigh bells and the merry laugh and song, as gay parties of young and old wend their way to and from each other's houses.

" Neither locks had to their doors, nor bars to their windows;
But their dwellings were open as day and the hearts of the owners;
There the richest was poor, and the poorest lived in abundance."

Happy the angler who, in his short respite from the harrassing cares of the busy world, finds his way among such pleasant pastures green.

Crowding the foothills closer, and near to the trail of the bush, are the homes of the trappers and guides. They form a class by themselves somewhere between the *habitan* and the Indian. They are the descendants of the old *coureurs de bois* and possess all the traits of their ancestors. Under the old French regime large numbers of the young men with a disinclination for honest labor in the fields, banded together in small parties and struck out into the wilderness to trade with the Indians for beaver skins, or to trap them on their own account. I have a suspicion that a too close ecclesiastical supervision, and frequent penance for the freaks of young blood, may have hastened their departure, but upon this point the records are silent. In vain did the Governor proclaim their proceedings illegal and threaten outlawry against them; equally vain the threats of excommunication thundered after them by the Jesuit fathers and the Recollets, the taste of the freedom and license of the camp-fire was far more potent, and defections from the ranks of the younger men in the colony still continued until it was estimated that over eight hundred of them were engaged in the "nefarious" pursuit of the beaver. Animated by a spirit of adventure, they penetrated the great unknown wilderness from the shores of the St. Lawrence to the Hudson's Bay. Many of them contracted alliances with the dusky maidens of the forests and acquired considerable influence in the councils of the tribes from which they took their squaws, and in time became almost as savage.

Once a year it was their custom to repair to one of the French towns. Francis Parkman thus describes the return of a party of these gentry from their rovings:

"Montreal was their harboring place, and they conducted themselves much like the crew of a man-of-war paid off after a long cruise. As long as their beaver skins lasted they set no bound to their license. The new-comers were bedizened with a strange mixture of French and Indian finery, while some of them, with instincts more thoroughly savage, stalked about the streets as naked as a Potawattamie or a Sioux. Drinking and gambling filled the day and night. When at last sober, they sought absolution from the priests and once more disappeared within the shades of the forest."

After the conquest of Canada the Hudson's Bay Company sprang into vigorous being, and the *Coureurs de bois* at once found their alloted place in its employ. Of late years the Company has dispensed with the services of many of these forest rangers, who have returned to the villages of their birth, and marrying, have settled down on a bush farm upon the edge of that wilderness they love so well. The domestic ties are not sufficiently strong to wean them from their first love. Old Jean Le Blanc is a good example of his race. When the frosts of autumn have tinged the mountains with a thousand dazzling hues Jean becomes uneasy and restless. At all hours of the day he may be observed at the corner of his little log house, that commands a view of the forests, blowing thick clouds of smoke from his short, black pipe, and taking observations. Some fine morning he is seen entering the edge of the bush, old flintlock under his arm, snowshoes slung over his shoulders, together with his small pack of traps and other necessaries. What becomes of him afterward no one knows; but early in the spring he reappears smelling strongly of smoke, and drawing behind him a very heavily laden traineau, the proceeds of his winter work, the skins of the caribou and moose that have fallen before old flintlock, and the pelts of beavers, minks and martins to his traps.

Jean is a good trapper, a poor shot ; he is full of the lore of the bush, but ignorant of everything else ; superstitious as the Indians among whom he has so long dwelt, and as full of omens, but considers himself a good Catholic ; cheerful and as light-hearted as a schoolboy, he is the guide *par excellence.*

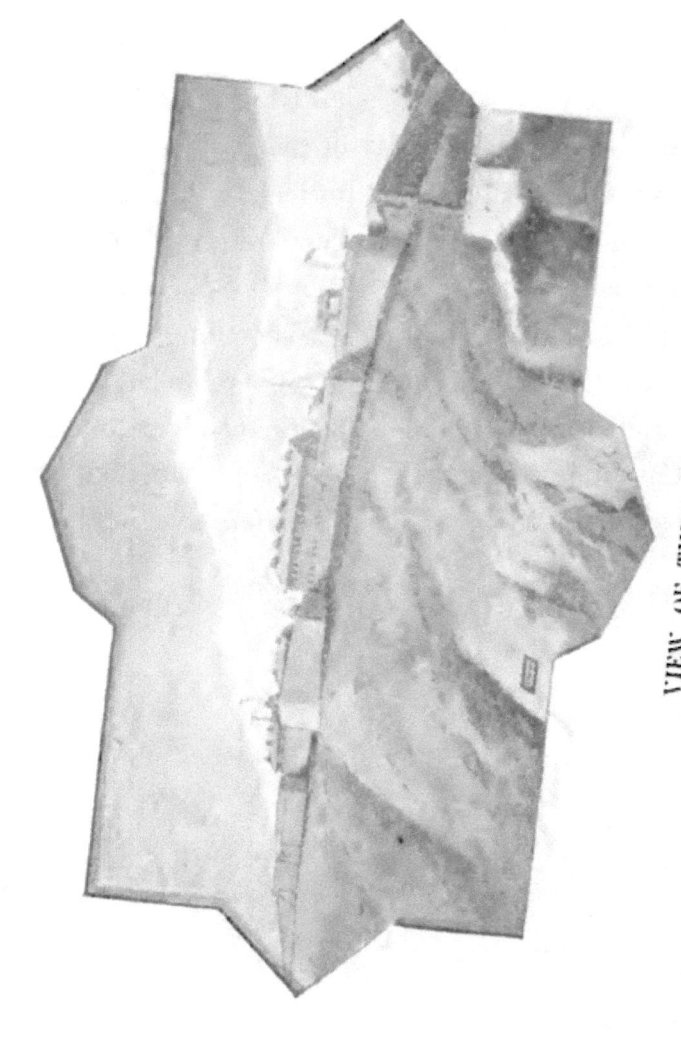

VIEW OF THE CITADEL.

CHAPTER SECOND.

QUEBEC--LAKE ST. CHARLES.

"O fortress city, bathed by streams
  Majestic as thy memories great,
  Where mountains, floods and forests mate
  The grandeur of the glorious dreams,
  Boon of the hero hearts, who died
  In founding here an Empire's pride!"

Chas. Farnham, who has written entertainingly of the varied phases of Canadian life, says of Quebec, that it is the Poet's Corner of America. I am not going to dispute the fact that there is everything in the life and history of the quaint old city to inspire a poet's muse, but I am going to add a sub-title to Mr. Farnham's to complete the full text, which now reads: "The Poet's Corner of America, and the Angler's Tryst." Where else on this broad continent do these knights errant of the rod and rifle so love to fore-gather in mighty council.

On the site of the old Chateau St. Louis, the former castle of the early governors from the warlike Frontenac, the representative of *le grand Monarque*, to the days of Lord Aylmer, the English vice-roy, now sits a stately pile of buildings known as the Chateau Frontenac Hotel, the great council-house of these modern seigneurs of the bush. From its turreted windows they command the boundary of their own domain as

CHATEAU FRONTENAC

they sit in cheerful conclave and plan expeditions for the collection of tithes from river, lake and forest. Theirs is a mission of peace and good will towards all conditions of men, and good fellowship the motto of their order.

In time they come to know this strangely curious

city and its storied past, and they love to linger within its gates and live in imagination the scenes of long ago. The romances of Gilbert Parker, of Wm. Kirby, and the chronicles of Jas. LeMoine have entered deep into their hearts. The many curious phases of life in the old French city are endowed with fresh interest with the new light of knowledge of the tragic and dramatic events which have centered in this early capital of European government on this continent.

The past is ever close to the present in this ancient stronghold, or rather I should have said, that the present ever recedes into the middle ages, and you are merely a spectator from some far away Altruria of what is transpiring about you, and you wander about in a mist of delightful sensations with a mind stored with its traditions and romance into which everything fits and becomes a part of this illusion. Convents, monasteries and churches jostle barrack, casemate and magazine, and the Citadel hovers above them all. The call of trumpets, the roll of drums for the morning inspection of troops are answered by the pealing of bells to remind the faithful of their religious duties. Nuns in solemn sober procession, priests clad in *surtanne* and high beavers, monks in strange garb, soldiers in gay trappings of war, sailors in blue, habitans in *étoffe du pays* and long beef moccasins, market women in short quilted skirt and big sun shades, make up the same street life as of yore. Big guns and little guns, long

CITADEL GATE.

guns and short guns, pyramids of shot and shell, massive walls and great stone gates, ditches and embankments recall the periods of seiges, assaults, repulses and conquest. There is a confusion of little, narrow, dark and crooked streets running up and down hill and bringing up abruptly and absurdly against some convent wall, or big gun platform, and the houses which line them are of high and low degree, but all pushing out into the thoroughfare for closer communion with the human life about them; but they are of another age, a period when the lily of France floated above the Castle St. Louis, and in the tradition and atmosphere of that regime their inhabitants still live, proud of their French descent, proud of their ancient language, laws, and institutions, true Britons in loyalty, but French at heart.

Directly beneath the Chateau Frontenac Hotel, and several hundred feet above the St. Lawrence, which washes the base of the cliff, is the Dufferin Terrace from which the panorama is surpassingly beautiful, nay grand. All anglers smoke. Let us therefore enjoy our after evening-dinner cigar while strolling along the favorite promenade. It is now in shadow, and the cool breeze of coming night invites to exercise. The setting sun floods the valley, lights the mountains and casts deep shadows in their valleys, crowns the tin spires and roofs of distant churches, sends dancing rays over the water to the Island of Orleans, whitens the sails of ships far out in the harbor, and then goes down in a burst of color that fairly pales a masterpiece of Turner's. We linger until the cold gray light of northern twilight proves the day has gone to rest.

On my angling pilgrimages to Canada I have invariably found that the week which I gave to Quebec was far too short. Every stone, street, bastion, convent and church possesses some historical interest, and the multiform life, and human interests past and present binds one to the scene, and after thirty years I find new pleasures, for I have tasted of the sweets of a warm-hearted hospitality, which a permanent residence now of some five years on the outskirts of the old stronghold, has not lessened.

Beautiful and fascinating as Quebec is, the eager longing to go-a-fishing tempts us to a day's outing on Lake St. Charles, a dozen miles from Quebec over a good road. It is to be a sort of preliminary skirmish with the trout, to warm the blood and steel the nerves preparatory to the greater campaign. In the early morn we drive out of the city across the Dorchester Bridge and up the Charlesbourg Road. Alexis is our carter. He is French of course, but with a voluble flow of curious English and a strange philosophy verging on to fatalism that keeps him in unfailing good humor with himself. His historical lore is somewhat mixed, but we make it a point to draw him out on all occasions.

The flush of early sunrise lights the valley, and the dew-drops clinging to every blade of grass reflect a thousand rays. Great fields of timothy wave gently in the light breeze. The sweet smell of cattle and white clover is borne on the air. Thin trails of smoke from wide-mouthed hospitable chimneys show these country people to be early risers even though we had other evidence in the fat, jolly looking *habitan* women jogging along on their way in to the city market, seated

HUCKSTER MAKING A BARGAIN

in the middle of their two wheeled cart with its square topped canvas roof, and surrounded by boquets of garden and wild flowers, little bunches of parsley and radishes, a dish of *boudin*, half a dozen spring chickens, some maple sugar, two or three dozen eggs, a few pairs of home knit socks, a piece of home made **catalagne** and other tiny odds and ends of a thrifty housewife's gathering, to be bargained away on the open market square amidst much chattering and gossip.

These virtuous and happy spouses are probably the direct descendants of those young damsels who were consigned to Canada at the instigation of Intendant Talon to become the wives of the soldiers of the *Carignan-Salières* regiment which had been disbanded in Canada in order to increase the number of settlers. Later, the Intendent writes to Colbert, and grows quite enthusiastic over the result of these marriages in the numerous offspring which was being added to the population of Canada. How well successive generations have maintained this reputation for fecundity is evidenced in every household you enter. Families of sixteen or eighteen are not unusual, while those of twelve or thirteen, which entitles the head of family to a bonus of one hundred acres of land from the Government, are of such frequent occurrence as to occasion no remark. I myself know one still blooming matron, fat, fair, and still in the forties, who has been the proud mother of twenty-two children, and she is not without hope that her husband may yet claim another Government grant.

But we have now reached the village of Charlesbourg with its great church, fine presbytery and big convent, and turning west follow along the crest of the upland that leads to the village of Lorette. Another panorama is unfolded of much pastoral beauty with the rugged gray rock of Quebec and its flaming min-

CITADEL OBSERVATORY.

arets, and the broad St. Lawrence as a background. Our roadway is macadamized and we bowl along in good style until we reach the *chemin de patate* that leads over the low mountain to the lake. The country is now rougher and the soil poorer, the houses and barns more diminutive, but in the countenances and air of the men and women we meet on the roadside there is an appearance of greater good nature and contentment. One old fellow we met driving a sorry little bull with patched harness, and a cart whose wheels were traveling at right angles to each other, but the world seemed very sweet to the old chap who was carolling "*A la Claire Fontaine*" in a high pitched key quite unmindful of our passing other than a, "*salut M'sieurs!*"

"Alexis, what do these people live on in the long winter?"

"B'gosh," Monsieur, "I tink dey must live h'on a chew h'of de gum, and a tune h'of de fiddle."

The less burdened the French-Canadian is with worldly possessions the more completely happy he is. "No cow no care" is his motto. Yet squalid poverty is unknown among them from the very simplicity of their living. Jean's clothes may be well patched, but he is never in rags; his little house may contain only the bare necessaries, but it is as white as whitewash can make it; the children run barefooted, but they get enough to eat to keep them fat and rosy. In the gathering twilight the sound of fiddle or accordian is heard in the land, and light hearts grow lighter to the air of *"La Canadienne."*

Lake St. Charles comes into view from the summit of the hill; a long winding sheet of bluest of blue water, the lower end in a small valley cultivated to the water's edge, the upper amidst broken mountains still

MARTELLO TOWER.

in all their wildness. We stop at the comfortable little hostelry of widow Stansfield in a grove of spruce and flowers.

The remainder of our day was full of quiet pleasure. We drifted idly about the lake, now and again taking a trout of moderate size. In the greater heat of the day we went ashore on a wooded point, boiled our tea over a little camp fire, smoked and discoursed of many things. Towards evening, in the shadows of the mountains, we rose and landed some few large fish, but that supreme angler's hour on these clear water lakes before the darkness we missed, for we had arranged to return to Quebec that same evening.

CHAPTER THIRD.

LAKE BEAUPORT.

> " Of recreation there is none
> So free as fishing, is, alone ;
> All other pastimes, do no less
> Than mind and body, both possess ;
> My hand alone my work can do
> So, I can fish and study too."

I once heard Henry Ranger, the artist, say that outside of Quebec no country in the world other, perhaps, than Holland could produce such cloud effects, and I believe him. The day we drove to Lake Beauport we were favored with an exhibition that aroused all our admiration. From out of the west and over the mountains there kept rolling out in rapid succession snowy, fluffy, floating, ragged fringed balls of varying sizes and depths, and the sun kept getting in among them and setting fire to their ragged borders which blazed up in yellows and reds and crimsons, leaving trails of pearl gray smoke. In time the vault of the sky was filled with these vapory forms moving in graceful stately *quadrilles d'honneur,* and over the landscape drifted their shadowy forms chasing the sunshine from place to place in laughing mood. One or two small clouds in the dark livery of mourning dropped silent tears upon the bosom of mother earth, but they were unnoticed in the general hilarity.

At Gaspard's we stop long enough to enjoy a hearty lunch served in mine host's best style. This is a famous rendezvous for Quebec's *jeunesse d'orée,* and in the long winters a sleighing party to Gaspard's, with supper and dance, is among the delightful events. There is an appearance of homely comfort about the establishment, and a quiet air of genuine hospitality that lends a charm to the picturesque old place in pleasant contrast to the average village or wayside inn on this continent, which is too often a dirty, ill kept house, with scant and saucy attendance.

We turn aside here to pay a flying visit to the ruins of the Chateau Bigot of unsavory name, around which tradition and romance have woven a story of woman's frailty and imprisonment, a man's lust and riotous dissipations, the murder of the woman, the final undoing of the man, who was sent to France, arrested, and tried for his many crimes against his King and country, a blending of facts and fiction somewhat difficult to disentangle even were I so inclined, but perish the thought, for ruinous chateaus with historical and romantic associations are far too scarce in our new world, and I am going to cling to my belief in all that is related of this one. Besides, does not the career of Francois Bigot, the last Intendant of France in Canada, supply the material for a score of dramatic romances sufficient to invest the chateau with rare interest, and unknown possibilities for the future novelist? Has not Gilbert Parker, with consummate genius, told a new story in his "Seats of the Mighty," and invested it with every appearance of reality? Is not the "Scarlet Woman" a possible successor in the chateau to the Algonquin maid?

I enquired our way to the ruins from an old woman who was gathering wild strawberries in a field near by.

With smiling alacrity and much volubility she offered to show us the way.

Her berry boxes were tubes of birch bark with bottoms sewed in. They were all gathered together for convenience of carrying by a flat knitted woolen string.

Would *Madame* sell her berries and boxes? Certainly, if *Monsieur* commands, and she would leave the price to him.

A silver fifty cent piece makes her eyes dance in her head, and the Commodore reaches out for the boxes, and is about to put them under the seat.

"Would *Monsieur* mind, but the boxes are tied together with my garters, and if we have no use for them?"

"What," exclaimed the Commodore, "are these garters," holding up the woolen strings before alluded to; "well, if Madam doesn't object to going without those appendages a while longer I would like to buy those self same garters to take home as a present to my wife"—and another quarter is handed out, and the Commodore's face is wreathed in smiles.

Honi soit qui mal y pense, but I'm going to hang these boxes and garters in my library in New York.

"And what about your wife Commodore?"

"Well I must wait until I get her," replied that suave dissimulator.

The severity of the climate in Canada does not

lend itself with gentle leniency to ruins. Two half destroyed gable walls, some piles of stone, among which the black alder and raspberry grew luxuriantly, were all that were left to mark the former site of profligate luxuriousness. During the blockade of Quebec in the winter of 1775-76 some of Benedict Arnold's troops occupied the Chateau, and it is the tradition that they set fire to it upon their departure, but such is not the case, for as late as 1834 it was in a fair state of preservation. In the early part of the century a club of *bon-vivants*, the "Baron's," frequently fore-gathered at the Chateau to re-enact the revelries of the days of Bigot.

With many exchanges of compliments with the old dame, we continued our journey to the lake.

The picturesque is rarely absent on the roadsides about Quebec.

At a gateway, leading into one of the low eaved farm-houses, stood a handsome black-eyed girl of eighteen with a complexion like a peach, and teeth of wondrous whiteness. She was dressed in a short blue home-spun linen *jupon*, beneath which showed a pair

4

of bright red stockings. A big alpine home-plaited straw hat covered a shapely head and was gathered in with a ribbon under a saucy chin. She held two frisky calves in leash while she made cheerful gossip with old Foy, the professional beggar, sitting in his dog wagon, and the dogs were enjoying a quiet loll in the dust with tongues extended.

BEGGAR AND DOG.

The Commodore raved over this picture the remainder of the day, and would not be comforted. It was evidently a case of love at first sight.

The mountains close in about Lake Beauport and it nestles cosily among them; a lovely little sheet of water of many headlands and bays. Several pretty summer cottages cling to the mountain sides, and the little hotel at which we put up, known as Bigaouette's, has a number of permanent summer boarders. It is well kept, and the proprietor anxious to afford every facility to visiting anglers in the way of boats and canoemen. Our guide's stories proved a great source of amusement to us in the intervals between a rise, strike, and a struggle, for the trout in this lake are the gamiest fish in Canadian waters, and as they run to a weight of $2\frac{1}{2}$ lbs., capital sport is to be had if the angler is expert and fertile in resources, for the water is clear, and the trout shy. We soon discovered that a shot on the casting line, and allowing the tail fly to trail well under water, was a most killing method during the early evening, but as the shadows deepened the fish rose to the fly on the surface for a short time, and then as suddenly stopped. We put up our rods, lighted our pipes, and listened to Gabriel's bear story as he paddled us down the lake in the moonlight.

H'all dese *montagnes* 'ere ver' fine place for bear. He com h'every summer tree, four mebbe, h'an sometime I catch him h'on de trap, udder time I shoot him. Wen I was boy, p'r'aps sixteen, my fadder giv me de gun wat he use h'on de Papineau war at St. Eustache. I'm ver' proud h'on dat gun, h'an wan day I say to

Philemon Gervais who 'av gun too: "Philemon we go shoot de partridge behin de beeg montagne wat you see." I go wan side, h'an Philemon he go h'on de udder. Bimby I com to beeg pine tree wat de wind brake h'in two bout twanty feet from grown. Dere

was planty scratches h'on dat tree, h'an when I look h'up I see dere was de beeg hole. I lak ver' well to see wat was h'in dat 'ole, h'an I go for fin a small dead spruce to put against de pine. Den I clim h'up de spruce h'an I look h'in de 'ole, but I aint see nudding, I reach h'over sum more, wen de wood she give way, h'an I fall down h'in dat tree. I fall h'on sumting dat sof, and I d'ont remenber h'any more for long time.

When I wake h'up I feel scar' h'almos to det, and someting sof was move near me, h'an I know dat h'it was some leettle bear. B'gosh! I yell and call for dat feller Philemon, h'an I'av fear dat I go be die h'in dat tree. Bim-by I 'ear noise h'on de bush h'an I yell sum more, h'an den I 'ear scratch, scratch. I look h'up to see de beeg mudder bear wid 'er 'ead lookin down h'at me. She turn roun for come down. Mon Dieu! I gone now for sure, but wan she got near I grab her bihine leg wid both hans, h'an I let a beeg yell. She run h'up dat tree like she mad, h'an I 'ol h'on tight, h'an yell sum more. Down de h'outside she go ver' quick h'an when she reach de grown I let go h'an de bear she run h'off in the bush, h'an I not stop till I get h'in my fadders 'ouse.

The sound of banjo and a deep bass voice floated over the water, and the song was:

"Slowly down the west the weary day is dying,
 Slowly up the east ascends the mellow mystic moon.
 Swift swoop the hawks; the hooting owls are flying,
 Through the darksome splendor breaks the lonesome cry
 [of loon."

A long mocking laugh of loon was the answer from far up the lake.

The drive back to town in the moonlight was not the least pleasant part of our day's outing.

QUIET REACH ON THE JACQUES CARTIER.

CHAPTER FOURTH.

THE JACQUES CARTIER RIVER.

"Above the waters' brink
 Hush'd winds make summer riot;
 Our thirsty spirits drink
 Deep, deep, the summer quiet."

There is no river in the Province of Quebec more famed in angling literature than the Jacques Cartier. It deserves all the encomiums passed upon it by sucessive generations of anglers for the magnificent trout which haunt its waters, and the varied and romantic scenery throughout its course. The lower valleys of the river were colonized many years ago by Scotch, Irish and English settlers, and some of their descendants yet remain on this outpost of civilization, but the mountains crowd down on the little valleys and forbid any extension into their domain, and the settlement has reached its limit. Shut in by the mountains on the one side, and crowded by the French parishes on the other, it has become a little world unto itself, with many strange customs and quaint traditions.

Scotch as a highland glen, as Irish as the lakes of

Killarney, as English as Yorkshire, and yet, a curious commingling of racial characteristics and national peculiarities which is all very interesting. The survival of the fittest has produced a hardy people to cope with the rugged conditions of life on this rough frontier, but they are hospitable and kindly to the stranger at their gate, and the word angler is an "open sesame" to their homes. In this valley reach of the river it twists and turns, frets and fumes, bubbles and gurgles, but is nowhere too rough for canoeing, and in the still reaches great trout lurk in the deep holes, but trout there are everywhere within its waters. Like all the northern tributaries of the St. Lawrence that take their source in the wild and sterile mountain region, the Jacques Cartier, flowing from the lake of the same name, for the first thirty miles of its course is a very rough river, everywhere impeded by chaotic rocks, and broken into dozens of falls, but as the mountains recede from its banks it subsides into a brawling river of many rapids, but canoeable.

In a subsequent chapter I shall have occasion to treat of the upper section of the river, and of the Great Lake Jacques Cartier.

Upon my return from Lake Beauport I found a letter awaiting me, from which I extract the following:

"River in excellent condition; Charles will come for you Wednesday."

Irresistible temptation!—a hasty oiling of rods, testing lines and flies, and looking up the other requisites, and Wednesday found me waiting the departure of Charles from his quarters, *Cote d'Abraham.*

"Now, come! pitch those traps of yours into the cart; time's up, and I can't wait while you sit there making eyes at Jane."

I hasten to comply with this peremptory request, and while arranging my traps sounds reach my ears, as though some one was engaged in a lively double-shuffle, and then Jane's voice, in tones of remonstrance, is heard: "Charley, you're a wretch, and if you attempt to kiss me again I'll send word to your wife."

"And I'll be the bearer for you!" I cried, as I entered the house. "That was a pretty excuse of his to get me out of the way! Charley, I'm ashamed of you—an officer in Her Majesty's service, and a married man!"

Further discussion is cut short by the appearance

of the cart at the door, and, waving a farewell, with a few flying compliments to the fair Jane, Charley puts whip to the horse and we are on the way from Quebec to Valcartier, distant eighteen miles. At Charlesbourg a rapid exchange of banter takes place between Charley and the pretty daughter of the postmaster in the choicest of Canadian French, and I am evidently being shown up by Charley as an eligible bachelor from the States looking for a Canadian wife.

Charley has seen life, tasted it in many phases, cast his bread upon many waters, and roving, gathered many experiences to exploit to interested audiences in the long winter evenings around his cheerful hearth on the banks of the Jacques Cartier. He fought his way to California in 1850, and pioneered many a gulch in seeking for gold. He crossed the Isthmus by the Nicaragua route, on his return to New York, to seek the gold fields of Australia. His adventures in the Antipodean gold fields, were fraught with romance, but after a few more years of wanderings in strange places, Charley returned to Canada.

We put the horse up for an hour at the Indian

village of Lorette, and while Charley is concocting a "back-bone stiffner" as he terms it, I amuse myself in wandering about among these degenerate descendants of the once mighty Hurons, and watching the various industries carried on by the men and squaws. They all savor of the primitive life of the Indian, but in the faces of men and women there is little trace remaining of their savage ancestors, and their village life is not unlike that of their French neighbors. They still maintain a tribal form of government, with their big chiefs and little chiefs. An Indian agent watches over their affairs, and the reservation is still jealously exclusive of the white man, unless he bears the name of Sioui, Groslouis, Gonzague *et cetera*, patents of original red blood.

The men, true, however, to the tradition of their noble progenitors, are still hunters and trappers, and of late years, also act as guides and canoemen to adventurous parties of anglers and sportsmen. In the intervals, which are spent in the bosoms of their families, they make snowshoes, tan skins for moccassins, build canoes, and swagger about the village. The women make the hundred and one prettily worked birch-bark constructions that are sold in Quebec, moccassins, and splint baskets, and bear a numerous progeny. The small chapel where they worship dates back to

HARD AT WORK.

1721. Crowning the heights above the valley of the St. Lawrence, and beside the river St. Charles, which now makes a mad leap into a deep chasm cut through the limestone, the little village posseses a decided picturesqueness, and is well worthy of a visit. I offered pennies to be shot at by young braves, with bows and arrows, and in the fulness of my good will towards all conditions of men and children, I ventured to hand a youngster of tender age a bright five-cent piece. He held it before his eyes, and then bolted it, but not soon enough to escape the argus eye of mama squaw.

Seizing the youngster, by what should have been the seat of his pants, she stood him on his head and proceeded to wollop him so vigorously that the coin soon made its appearance.

Great excitement and interest on the part of the crowd. Great rejoicing on mama squaw's part on recovering the coin.

"She'm bad boy, swal heap much mone," exclaimed an old squaw.

Last summer, when at Lake St. John, I visited the Indian village. Meeting a good squaw with papoose on her back, I said :

"Little Indian," at the same time chuckling the youngster under the chin ?

" Yes, lilly injin, lilly injineer."

Late in the evening, seated in the comfortable little smoking-room of my old friend and companion *du bois* enjoying my cigar, I listen with a sympathetic ear to his report of a bad attack of rheumatism that has placed him *hors du combat*, though with his accustomed kindness and forethought, everything is prepared for my enjoyment and sport. "Suppose you fish down the river to-morrow," suggests my friend, "for since the dam was built at the head of the falls it has thrown the water back for several miles, and there are some immense fish lurking about the deep pools between here and Sullivan's."

The morning dawned a little too bright, but there was a good stiff breeze blowing, which in part made amends. Douglas, my old guide and canoe-man, was early on hand, and advised taking the small flat as more comfortable to fish from, and as I entertain a profound respect for mine ease, I had a high-back chair placed in the prow. A bountiful lunch provided by the girls is safely stowed away, our anchor shipped, and we slowly drift along. The river just here is extremely beautiful in its meanderings among the hundreds of lovely little elm-covered islets, and from its lake-like appearance. Our noiseless movements are only interrupted by the occasional rise of a trout at my flies, and the sudden and mysterious transfer of the same to the creel, or the plunge of a kingfisher into the water and his noisy chattering as he flies to his perch on some dead limb overhanging the banks, there to wait and watch another opportunity to procure his breakfast. Feeling compelled to keep one eye on us while the other goes hunting, he has missed his mark several times. It was just in a bend of the river, beneath a high, precipitous bank, that I observe, close in shore, a heavy swirl, but supposing it to be caused by a muskrat, I at first paid no attention to it until it was repeated, when I discover my error. Douglas brings the canoe to a stand, and I perceive the reason for the fish's singular appearance in this most unlooked-for of places. Above the bank was a field of grass, and every moment or so a grasshopper would over-jump his mark and fall into the water, that moment to be sucked in by a trout. My fly-book contains an imitation and I re-fashion my leader. A long cast neatly made, and in a second the hook is firmly fastened in the jaws of a two-pound fish. A rapid run or two, some lofty tumbling, and my trout is safely landed. Again did I try a cast in there and with precisely the same result—another two-pound fish. There were no more, and never again did I take a trout near that spot, big or little.

Last summer a friend and I were fishing the river, when the following occurred: My friend, who was grubbing it with a worm on the bottom, felt a tug on his line; he struck, and a magnificent trout broke the surface of the water a second afterwards, apparently well hooked. My friend played it until he thought it safe to bring it alongside the boat for me to land. I took the line, but the moment the full weight of the fish came I felt something give way, and I landed, not the trout, but a two-inch gudgeon as lively as a cricket. The gudgeon had gorged the worm and hook, and a second afterwards the trout came along and bolted the gudgeon. The hook being buried in the gudgeon, there was nothing to hold the trout.

Moving along slowly, as the fish rise less frequently to my fly, conversation becomes more animated. The fol-

lowing yarn, which Douglas related to me, will bear repeating:

"Well, sir, one night after young Pat came to camp, he says suddenly to me, 'Douglas, I'm going to catch one of those mocking devils of loons; they've hung around my raft all day, hooting and diving, until sorra a fish could I take.'

"I wish you luck, Paddy, my boy," says I, laughing, for I thought it was joking the fellow was; but next night, when I got back to camp, Paddy was there, and looking as proud and as satisfied as you please, for, by the powers! he had a loon, and the old father-bird at that, and this was the way he took him. He caught a small minnow near the shore and baited it on a large, strong hook, to which he tied a line about a hundred feet long, with the other end of the cord fastened to a good-sized block of wood, and off he starts. Presently, down comes the loons.

"'Ho! ho! ho! whoa!' cries the old fellow.

"'Faith,' says Pat, 'you'll soon change your tune,' making ready his line and slowly circling round the loons until he was half-way, when he began to pull in his line right across the track of the old bird, who gives a startled look at first, and then laughs a quiet laugh at his being so nervous like, and takes a good squint at the fish slowly swimming away in front of him, and then makes a rush for it. Paddy strikes hard, and then pitches the float overboard. The loon lets out an awful yell, and down he goes, but the float soon pulls him up. In the end Paddy knocks him on the head. He thinks that was the best morning's sport he ever had."

"A very remarkable catch, certainly, Douglas. I am glad you were there to vouch for the truth of it."

"Halloo! this is the first smolt I have taken in the Jacques Cartier for two years. Since the dam was built at the falls it has presented an almost insurmountable obstacle to even the more active salmon that have overcome the formidable falls at Dayree's. I have been laughed at for years for maintaining that salmon ever ascended above Sullivan's falls, but I know well-authenticated instances of their capture by the settlers along the river; and have not I taken their progeny in countless numbers in times past? The heavy flood of last year has brought a few salmon up again, as this smolt testifies."

"Douglas, who is that standing on the opposite bank? Old Dulkin, is it not? Let us steer in there and have a chat with the old fellow."

"Well, Dulkin, how are you?"

"Och, by my sowl, and is it your honor? And it's a proud day for me, so it is, to shake your honor's hand. It was your father, sir, God bless him! that was good to me, and many's the lift he's given me coming from town, and a wee drop of the cratur."

Here is a hint. It won't do for the present generation to be outdone by the former; "Dulkin, here's something that will help you climb the mountain to-night."

The old man's eyes sparkle as he takes the cup, and with "Here's to your honor's health," he gulps down a good gill of whisky without so much as winking.

I am sorry to add that Dulkin's reputation for veracity is questioned, but he is such a plausible, wily, old fellow that he would deceive a saint. A few years ago he had all the officers of the garrison out here, from the gallant Colonel Strange, the Commandant, down to the lieutenant, hunting bears, though it turned out to be a wild-goose chase for them and a perfect godsend for Dulkin, who for several months afterward lived like a lord off their liberality. I hardly need say that not a bear had been seen near Dulkin's place, but the old man's fertility in resources to raise the wind took him to town with wonderful stories of

DULKIN'S HOUSE.

the bears that were depleting the ranks of his sheep, and praying for succor. The truth leaked out, and it was long before the participators in the hunt heard the last of Dulkin's bears.

I have often remarked that trout, without any accountable reason, and with great unanimity of action, will suddenly stop rising, and the most tempting flies will utterly fail to lure them from the bottom, and even though you shift your ground, yet the result is the same. "Douglas, do you see that birch whose low-reaching branches will furnish us a pleasant shade from the sun? There will we tie our boat, and until the trout change their minds again, we will indulge in a smoke and quiet meditation, for the work of this past hour has been quite exhausting."

Lulled by the gentle breezes that steal under our leafy covert and the soft ripple of the water against the boat, I drift fast into that delightful angler's dreamland, when there breaks upon my ear the sweet voice of some fair wood nymph, evidently approaching the river near our place of concealment, singing to herself the old Scotch ditty:

"Last May a braw wooer came down the lang glen,
 And sair by his love he did deave me.
 I said there was naething I hated like men,
 The deuce gae wi' 'm to believe me, believe me,
 The deuce gae wi' 'm to believe me."

Our enchantress, a pretty, rosy-cheeked girl of

eighteen, dressed in a short petticoat, and barefooted, hatless, with her wavy, light brown hair tied in a loose knot, rendered her a fitting ideal for the Highland lassie of "Burns." Dipping her pail full of water, she

returns up the bank unconscious of our presence. Waiting until her song died away in the distance we pushed out into the stream again.

The loss of our anchor and part of our rope cable brings to my mind a predicament I got in last year on the river that might have resulted seriously. A mile or two below Roche Platte the river contracts to about half its usual width, with a very heavy rapid. There are always a few fine trout to be taken at the foot of this rapid, but in order to fish it you must anchor at the head of it. On this particular day, when we came to pull up anchor, it resolutely refused to be budged an inch in spite of our tugging. Here was a pretty mess, and Etienne and I looked at each other in dismay.

"Etienne, this is a bad job. What are we going to do?"

"Sacrè! me not know; for sure go be die."

"You swim?" imitating the motion.

"No; me go down like what you call dam stone."

Umph! So much for having a chain, fastened with a staple, instead of a rope. "Here, you black rascal, crawl back and let me get there!" For two mortal hours did I saw at that chain with my bush knife and then with Etienne's before we were released from our dangerous berth.

"Douglas, my boy, did you see that rise? Now, gently, and I'll see how he likes this professor, or red hackle. There, so, that will do. I knew it; the red hackle against the field in this river. A four-pounder, Douglas, without a doubt, and well hooked. Softly, softly, my speckled beauty! not too many such somersaults, though I love dearly occasionally to see your fine form and mottled sides. The landing-net, Douglas, and see to it that you get it well under him. Oh! my charmer, kick away there in the creel, you can do no harm, for your hours are numbered! To-morrow you shall grace the table of the curé, and fill him with envy of my prowess, if so genial and open-hearted a man is capable of such a feeling. Now, Douglas, turn the prow of our boat homeward, for I have had sport enough for one day. I will not give the number of the slain nor the weight, for are not all such statistics said to be born of the brain of the angler? But the Jacques Cartier forever!"

The Cook

CHAPTER FIFTH.

LAKE ST. JOSEPH.

"But yet, though while I fish I fast,
I make good fortune my repast;
And thereunto my friend invite,—
In whom I more than that delight,—
Who is more welcome to my dish,
Than to my angle was my fish."

An hour by train, or four hours by buckboard, is the distance to Lake St. Joseph, whatever that may be in miles. I like that good old fashioned *habitan* method of reckoning distances by pipes. It leaves much to the pipe, and to the imagination if you are not a smoker, but everyone smokes in French Canada, even the very small boy you meet on the roadside has a long clay pipe stuck in the corner of his mouth. The farmers grow their own tobacco, but cure it so badly that it is rank poor stuff, and they call it *frisé* because it makes your hair curl to smoke it, and your nose curl to smell it.

For the angler who likes his ease, a fair share of good fishing, cheerful companionship after a day on the water, and a feather bed to invite sound slumber, Lake St. Joseph is a very elysium. It is a lovely sheet of water of noble dimensions, wooded shores, and fine firm sand beaches. There are several comfortable little hostelries which harbor a goodly company of guests in the summer season, and a tiny steamer plies between them and the railroad station, and makes tours of the lake. Canoemen familiar with the lake will put the angler on the good fishing spots either for trout or black bass, this latter fish being very abundant in this lake and affording famous sport. Tuladi, or lunge, are also denizens of its waters and reach a size of 35 lbs.

I confess to a keen enjoyment in driving about the country near Quebec, and if after the macadamized roads are abandoned, the dirt roads are no better than elsewhere, a good buckboard makes easy journeying. It must be in the early morning when all nature is instinct with the life of the opening day, and the slowly rising mists in the valleys leave wooded islands in fairy lakes, from which come the sweet melody of bird matins, and the odors of pastured meadows. In these high latitudes the summer day breaks soon upon the closing night, but in the short intervening hours the northern breeze has swept over miles of forest covered mountain and comes laden with cool balsamic ozone, as exhilarating as champagne.

I believe that I expressed some such sentiments to my old friend, Jas. M. LeMoine, Esq., Quebec's famed historian, who had kindly offered to accompany me on a drive to Lake St. Joseph, but when I proposed four a.m. as our time of departure he perceptibly winced, yet offered no word of remonstrance, and it was so settled. Driving down the long wooded avenue leading to the charmingly situated sylvan retreat of my companion *du voyage*, beautiful " Spencer Grange," I recalled Kirby's lines :

> "I love Quebec for these good reasons, one,
> Her matchless beauty that so takes the eye,
> Her famous history in the years gone by,
> And last for sake of him, her worthy son,
> Bone of her bone, whose facile pen has run
> Through tomes of legendary lore that vie
> Wi h what the world loves best ; and so love I
> Quebec for these good reason, and upon
> The plinth of Wolfe and Montcalm lay my hand,
> And call to witness all the varied land
> Seen from the lofty capes embattled coigne,
> Mountain and vale and river, isles that gleam
> Resplendent with the memories that beam
> Upon them from the pages of LeMoine."

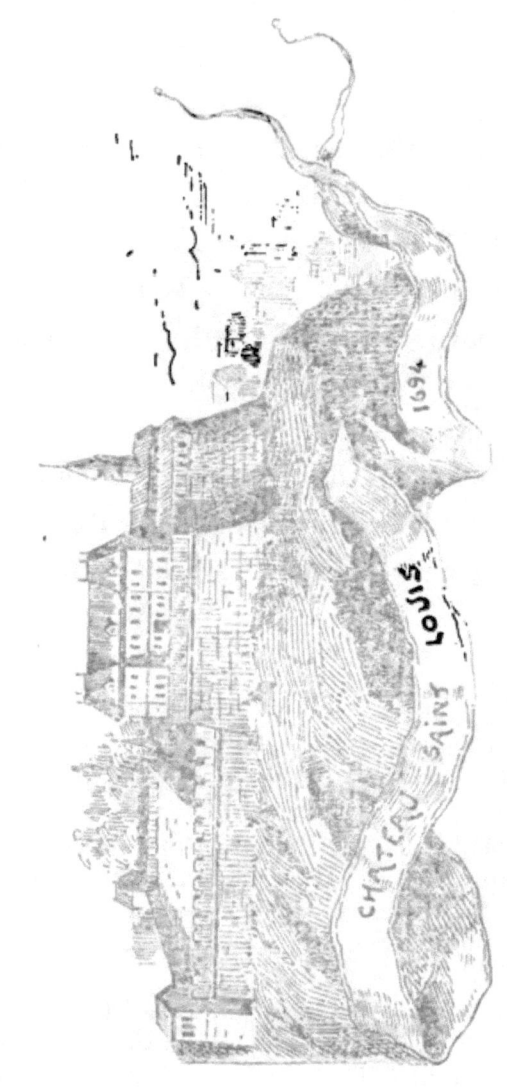

Some thirty or forty published volumes upon the history, archæology, botany, ornithology, fisheries, chase, and the legendary lore of the Province of Quebec attest the varied accomplishments and industry of Mr. LeMoine. He is the most approachable and genial of men, as hundreds of visiting knights of the rod will certify to.

I do not know that we selected the most direct route to the lake, but we chose a most picturesque and interesting one through some of the old settled parishes, and then over the mountain of *Bel-Air* on an unfrequented road through a wild bush down upon a sandy plain, long since deserted by its former inhabitants, until we reached the little church of the parish of St. Catherine, on the southerly bank of the River Jacques Cartier. We crossed the river on a flat bottomed scow drawn by a wire cable and windlass, and thence after a short drive we reached the lake in time to partake of a hearty dinner.

Some of the incidents of our pleasant journeying are recorded in my journal.

At St. Foye's, Mr. LeMoine pointed out an old earth work erected by the American troops under Gen.

Montgomery in 1775. They wintered here, and when smallpox broke out the church was converted into a hospital. Tradition asserts, that a soldier who was dying asked for a priest, but his request was denied. In the spring after the snow was gone, a *habitan* passing the grave saw an arm and hand uplifted. With the instinct of humanity, he procured a spade and duly replaced the exposed members in mother earth; but to his astonishment, upon passing the same spot the following morning, the arm and hand were again outstretched. Terrified at such an occurrence, he at once informed his neighbors, and together they went to consult *M'sieur le Curé*. After pondering some moments over so remarkable an incident, he announced his intention of proceeding to the grave to put at rest the uneasy spirit. Taking with him a small crucifix he placed it in the open hand, which immediately closed upon it, and uttering a prayer for the repose of the soul of the dead, the arm and hand were again reverently interred, and the troubled spirit was at rest.

I remarked that an unlettered people were great lovers of the marvellous, and that their folk lore was richest in extravagent legends, tales, and superstitions.

"It is peculiarly so among the French Canadians," said Mr. LeMoine, "and were I young again, I should devote myself to rescuing much that will soon pass away. Abbé H.-R. Casgrain has done something in this direction in his 'Legendes Canadiennes,' but there still remains an interesting field of research for the explorer. Dr. Prosper Bender, of Boston, probably, possesses the most complete knowledge for such a work and I believe that he intends some day to publish one."

"The long winter evenings among the *habitans*," continued Mr. LeMoine, "are devoted to *veillée* at each others houses. The *conteurs* of the parish are the honored guests, and are called upon to exploit the supernatural, the *loup-garou, lutin, feu-follet, sorcier, la jongleuse*, until the audience is fairly spell-bound and terrified with vague fears, or some fantastic story is told clothed in all the wealth of imagery and exaggeration the *conteur* is capable of imparting to it until his hearers fairly shriek with laughter. The *chanteur* also comes in for a share of the popular favor, especially if his repertoire includes a goodly number of the old romances and *complaintes* sung to the accompaniment of the accordion with which every Canadian house is supplied."

"Many years ago," said I, "an American journal published a series of articles on the songs of French Canada with translations of many of them. Apart from those of undoubted French origin, the Canadian songs are many of them valuable as pictures of the life of these simple peasants. The author of "*Le petit bois de l'Ail*" deserves immortality. He commences by alluding to the fact that there is a whole regiment of drunkards in the parish, of which he, Francois Juneau, merchant, is captain. With amusing inconsequence he then continues :

> "Upon one Sunday night,
> In pleasant summer weather
> When we went out to walk
> Francois and I together,
> At old man Gauthier's house
> The evening there we spent,
> And there came to pass
> The following strange event."

His audience being now prepared for a catastrophe, he proceeds to sketch a *veillée* :

"Well so I lit my pipe,
 As is my usual way,
 And to the folk of the house
 A few words did I say,
 To Delima I said :
"Will you permit me to
 Draw further from the rest
 So as to draw nearer you ?"

"Ah, yes indeed, with much
 Pleasure" then answers she,
 'If you have come to-night
 'Tis but to laugh at me.
 You far to faithless are
 To talk of love to me ;
 The one you always love
 Is your little Jerimie."

The bard now "returns" to a subject which he had never remotely hinted at, and draws a veil of provoking mystery over all the occurrences of the evening:

"To return to the old man.
 Out comes his night-capped head.
 At the top of his voice he says :
"Lima be off to bed !
 You who dwell in the town,
 Suburbs, or parish away,
 Withdraw immediately,
 For it is almost day."

> "I don't let the old man
> This for a second time say,
> So to François I said :
> Do you come home my way ?
> Good night my Delima
> I cut my lucky, and
> Bareheaded I go home,
> With my hat in my hand."

Thus with Wordsworthian simplicity is told the tragedy of " *Le Petit bois de l'Ail.* "

" *The Bal chez Boulé* " is another of those truthful pictures of Canadian life, with an absurd climax. " *Dans les chantiers nous hivernons* " depicts the daily life of the lumberman in the shanties. When the ballad is descriptive it hastens to its conclusion, the action is direct, the language simple. Where incidents are introduced they are either conventional or impossible.

That portion of our road that lay through the parish of *St. Augustin* clearly showed a thrifty and well-to-do population. Many of the houses were of pressed brick fronts, while the barns and outbuildings were numerous and spacious. The growing crop was mainly hay, timothy of rich growth. Large herds of cows grazed on the upland meadows. Every farm had its spring or stream flowing through it. Before a dairy a large Newfoundland dog on a treadmill worked a churn. He had no time to turn to look at us, or to

utter a bark, but continued steadily at his demnition grind. A merry party of youngsters in a buckboard drawn by a quiet sedate little bull passed us on their way berrying. We halted at a spring that looked cool and inviting, and had an amusing conversation with an old dame who came along.

"If the *Messieurs* would stop at the next house they would be heartily welcome to some fresh milk. She lived there with her daughter Liza, who had married Hilarion Gendron, and she had a hand loom in the house, and perhaps the *Messieurs* would like some *catalagne* (hand made rag carpet) made, or some *toile* (linen)?"

"Thank you, no," replied Mr. LeMoine, "my friend here is from the States, New York, and we are going a-fishing."

"What, the *Monsieur* from the States," why then turning to me, "I must know her son well; Flavien Travail, who works in the brick yards near St. Louis."

I replied that I hadn't the pleasure of knowing her son Flavien, and that St. Louis was some twelve hundred miles from New York.

This statement we could see made a bad impression, and the old lady plainly regarded me as an impostor, not an American at all, but *un Anglais*.

I partly appeased her, however, by purchasing a very handsome homespun, hand-woven linen apron in colored stripes that she wore, for which I paid the munificent sum of twenty-five cents.

After turning off the main road to cross the mountain we passed through some rough poor country. About mid-way, in a long swampy *sapin* bush, we came to a small clearing in which, struggling for existence, was a patch of half drowned oats, some drills of submerged potatoes, while in a field over-grown with ferns grazed a diminutive cow and a few ragged sheep. Further on we espied a log cabin, and a shed that evidently served for a barn. Before the door of this primitive abode a man was chopping some balsam wood. Drawing rein, I enquired my way, and finding I was on the right road, we entered into conversation.

"My friend," said I, "this appears to be a poor place for a man to settle."

"Ah no! Monsieur is mistaken, the land here is very fine."

"But," said I, "it is half under water."

"That," replied he, "is because we have had so much rain this summer, but *Monsieur* should see how dry it is when there has been no rain for a long time."

"Did you have a good crop of oats last year?" I asked.

"*Monsieur* should have seen my oats last summer; there was never anything to beat them, but the frost came so early that they were frozen before they ripened and I had to feed them to the cow."

"Well, your hay crop made up the loss of your oats?"

"*Mon dieu*, such hay, it was waist high, but while we were away for a few days to attend the wedding of my wife's sister, the cow and the sheep broke into it, and when we returned it was all tramped down."

"And your potatoes, how did they turn out?"

"I had a magnificent crop, but the pits filled with water from a great rain which came in the early winter, and they rotted."

"What did you do my good man to tide you over the long winter?"

"Why *Monsieur*, I cut cedar rails to sell, but if the good Lord is gracious I shall have good crops this year, and then we will do well. It is a fine place, that is when the summers are not too wet."

I handed him a quarter to be distributed among the half dozen sturdy little tow heads who had drawn around us, and drove on.

"There," exclaimed Mr. LeMoine "is an example of contentment with one's lot, and exemplifies the old song":

"Sol Canadien, terre chérie
Par des braves tu fus peuplée."

Another cabin which we passed had several pairs of caribou horns nailed over the door, but its sporting occupant was absent, probably gone a-fishing, and we couldn't blame him; there was nothing cheerful or inviting about his location, but I have never found one of his class whose civilized surroundings were much better. When the life of the bush gets into a man's whole system he has heart or eyes for nothing else.

After crossing the Jacques Cartier we turned aside from our road to take a look at the old manor house of the Seigniors Duchesnay. It is built of red brick, and of quaint design. It overlooks the river, and close beside it is a brawling stream that drives the banal mill, but the ancient glory of these old manor houses is departed. The only remnant of the feudalism of the past is the *cents et rentes* payable to the seignior at Martinmas.

"The seignorial tenures," remarked Mr. LeMoine, "were most curious, in the conditions imposed upon both seignior and *censitaire*. The seignior received a grant of wild land from the King on condition that he should put settlers upon it. He had to preserve the oak timber for shipbuilding, and the red pine for the manufacture of tar, and to notify the King's agents if he found minerals on the seigniory. He had to go through the form of paying homage and fealty to the King's representative at Quebec when he entered on possession, sometimes oftener, and to pay a fifth of the purchase money, if he sold the estate, to the royal coffers, though he was allowed a rebate of two-thirds for cash down. The *censitaire* or *habitan*, who held land under the seignior, had to pay the annual *cens et rentes*, often a *sol* (cent), or half a *sol*, with half a pint of wheat or a few live capons or eggs for each arpent. The land of the *censitaire* passed to his heirs, but in case he sold during his lifetime, the *lods et ventes* came into play and one-twelfth of the purchase money went to the seignior. By the *droit de retrait* the seignior could compel a purchaser within forty days of the sale to transfer the property to him at the price paid if he thought it had not fetched enough. The *censitaire* had to get his wheat ground at the seignior's mill, and on some seigniories to have his bread baked at the seignior's oven, paying a toll in each case; to give a tithe of the fish he caught to the seignior, to do *corvée* or road work, and to get out stone and timber for public purposes."

Mrs. Douglas, who manages the little hotel at the lake, made us most comfortable. Mr. LeMoine met some agreeable Quebec friends, and remained with them, and I went a-fishing for black bass, but with a trout rig in reserve.

The black bass, at all times a game fish, becomes the very incarnation of a fighter in the cold water of these northern lakes. I caught my first fish off a little wooded point shortly after we started, and although it only proved to be about 1½ lbs. in weight when landed, yet it gave me more sport than a fish twice its size in more Southern waters.

A little bay into which tumbled a tiny cold brook elicited from my canoeman the remark: " Ver' good place for *la truite Monsieur*." I change rods and after some patient casting and several changes of flies I take a couple of medium sized fish.

And so, moving along and with alternate rods I pick up a bass or a trout, and listen with interest to

the stories of my man, of the wonderful skill and success of some of *les Messieurs* from Quebec who come to fish the lake. I am afraid that my modest showing would have paled before the creels of those worthy disciples of the rod, but I had a glorious afternoon on the water, and when the sun went down in a great burst of splendor over the mountains amidst some clouds, I felt that the day had not been in vain.

TOURILLI LODGE.

CHAPTER SIXTH.

IN THE KINGDOM OF THE TOURILLI CLUB.

> "No cares or business here disturb our hours,
> While underneath these shady, peaceful bowers.
> In cool delight and innocence we stray,
> And midst a thousand pleasures pass the day.
> Sometimes upon a river bank we lie,
> When skimming swallows o'er the surface fly ;
> Just as the sun declining, with his beams
> Kisses, and gently warms the gliding streams ;
> Amidst whose current, rising fishes play,
> And roll in wanton liberty away."

When I. Emerson Palmer, kindest hearted, most genial of all good sportsmen, wrote to me and said "I am weary, shall we go a-fishing?" I felt the force of his appeal, for I knew that for months past he had been engaged in perfecting some machine which was to do what no machine had ever done before, one of the many clever inventions which has given him fame and fortune, and added to the world's progress, so I wired back: "Yes, and at Tourilli. Meet me Quebec June 4th."

To an over taxed brain Nature's remedy—rest—is nowhere found but in the solitude of these great North woods. A few weeks of canoeing, camping and fishing restore the exhausted vitality, and renew the waste of gray matter to the brain. He is wise who hearkens in time to the warning of the inward monitor, and goes a-fishing.

Somewhere about 1888 or '89 Commodore J. U. Gregory, of Quebec, Geo. Van Felson, and E. A. Panet, N. P., of St. Raymond, secured from the Provincial Government, under lease, the East and West branches of the St. Anne's River, the Tourilli River, and all the lakes and streams thereto contributary from their sources in the North to the limit of the settled parishes to the South. "The Tourilli Fish and Game Club" was duly formed and incorporated, and a limited number of Canadians and Americans admitted to membership. The aim of its founders was to make it the most complete organization of its kind, and with a high entrance fee of $250.00, with annual dues of from $25 to $50, to secure only members who could aid in carrying out the aims of its promoters. Their domain was a princely one, some one hundred square miles, the greater portion an unexplored wilderness, and to render this accessible to the members involved a large expenditure of money.

What has been accomplished in this direction is ably set forth in the report of the Secretary, Mr. Geo. Van Felson, for 1894, a pamphlet of some 35 pages.

Tourilli Lodge, the main camp, is situated on the main branch of the St. Anne River, about thirteen miles from St. Raymond, the beginning of the Club's limits on this branch of the river. It is of noble proportions and stands like the old Rhinish Castles on a spur of a mountain with the brawling river below, and a great wall of verdure covered mountains on the opposite shore. Hoary old birches dot the hillside to the river, and wild flowers cover the ground beneath their shade. Down the narrow river valley cluster the little log cabins of the guardian and guides, and the tiny farm buildings belonging to the club. Up the valley nothing but forest and rugged outline of mountain.

As is fitting, the club house is built massively of solid spruce logs, with a great stone chimney and ample fire place in the large living room. Twenty guests find roomy accommodation, and sixteen guides can also be provided for. If the interior decorations and appointments are not quite equal to the Waldorf's, the comfort is greater, and exquisite cleanliness prevails. Madame Lessard, the steward's wife, and the cook is an accomplished artist in her department and presents the guests with a daily *menu* of delicacies of surprising variety. She waits upon them in a snowy white apron, with gentle and smiling apology in quaint English that she hasn't more at her command to tempt the *messieurs* appetite, and if after the fifth or sixth course there is a cessation of hostilities, for even an anglers's appetite has a limitation, madame will suggest that coffee be served on the verandah. A spacious store house enables the members to supply all their wants for a short or long cruise in the bush, even to champagne or Reina Victorias, if inclined for such luxuries.

Thirty-six miles from Tourilli Lodge, in the depth of the wilderness, with no other means of access than by canoe and trail, is Camp George, another charming rustic lodge on the shores of Lake George, containing every necessary appointment, even to a store house, and will accommodate 12 guests. It cost $1600, but as windows, doors, sashes, nails, lime, stoves and furniture had to be patiently hauled over the trail in winter on hand sleds, employing 24 men almost the entire season, it cannot be considered an extravagant outlay. This camp is situated at the head of the Rivers Tourilli and St. Anne, on a table land which is covered with lakes, big and little, not one half of which are even known. Only last season an adventurous

PORTAGING ON THE TOURILLI RIVER.

member discovered one over seven miles long. I am not certain that they may not yet find another Lake Mistassini hidden away on the limits. The number of lakes actually known is bewildering, but those yet awaiting a discoverer must be legion. Every member of the club might have a river, several streams, and a score or so of lakes placed at his sole disposal, and there would still remain several hundreds just for friends. The management lays out forty or fifty miles of new trails yearly, merely to give the members an infinite choice of country. It has built good substantial log camps in twenty different localities, and each is fitted out with stoves, chairs, tables, and kitchen kits. Bark canoes, boats, and Gaspe canoes, to the number of sixty, are placed on rivers and lakes. Eighteen tents are also distributed among the camps to allow members an opportunity for further exploration and adventure. A large kennel of spaniels is kept for those who are fond of partridge shooting in the fall. I believe that in the dreams of some of the managers for the future of the club is an electric car service to connect all the rivers and lakes, but, as it is, I consider it the most fully provided for organization of its kind in the Province of Quebec, and instead of its present membership of fifty it should have at least one hundred.

Palmer arriving promptly on time by the Quebec Central enabled us to take the train on the Quebec and Lake St. John R.R. the same afternoon. An hour

and a half's ride brought us to the village of St.
Raymond, at the forks of the St. Anne River, where we
debarked. Several hundred people were gathered at
the station to see the train arrive, and there was much
speculation as to who we were, and whence we were
going, but there was nothing rude or obtrusive about it.
Railroads and strangers are yet novelties in the parish,
and take the place of the newspaper.

Ferdinand Godin, the club guardian, took charge
of our baggage and the two extra Indian guides we
brought with us from Lorette, and Palmer and I took
possession of a last century buckboard for the long
drive in the gathering twilight.

The river valley is exceedingly beautiful, an amphi-
theatre of successive tablelands, all well cultivated. The
dull roar of the river is ever within sound; often we
skirt its banks for long distances, and the moonlight
softly shimmering through the trees upon the broken
waters, produces a weird scene of wild beauty.

Madame Lessard expected us; a glorious little supper at 10 p.m. proved so, Commodore Gregory expected
us, and had remained this one night longer to bid us
welcome, and to make merry a long evening sitting

around the fire of logs in the big chimney. The genial author of "*En Racontant*" has had experiences as extended as his jurisdiction in the Department of Marine and Fisheries, and that I believe reaches to the Straits of Belle Isle, on the Labrador coast. I cannot forbear repeating one of the amusing stories of the Commodore's, told us that night.

"It was once my misfortune," said the Commodore, "to entertain a very distinguished savant, and he was for ever bringing conspicuously to my attention my extreme ignorance of many of the ologies by questions abruptly put, to which I could only make answer, that I really was not informed on the subject in question. I finally had to explain that since early youth I had had to devote my energies to other pursuits, but that in my official career I had acquired some knowledge of our Canadian birds and fishes."

"Umph!" replied this distinguished man, "I know the American birds very well, and many of them I can name from their song."

"For an outing, and some fishing, I took him to Lake St. Charles. We had the outing, but no fishing, for the water was like a mirror."

"The song of a bird in the bush attracted my friend's attention, and he quite correctly said, 'that is the hermit thrush?' A little later another song is heard of quite a different kind."

"I somewhat maliciously asked him if he knew the name of that bird."

"Why yes, quite well, that is the—the—well, really, the name has escaped me for the moment. What do you call it Mr. Gregory?"

"That, Sir, is the Irish nightingale, a bird without feathers, in other words, a bull frog."

"And that," said the Commodore, "was my sweet revenge."

The following morning Palmer and I stowed ourselves and our impedimenta in two Gaspe canoes, and with two capable canoemen to each, father and son in both instances, we commenced the difficult ascent of the river, which is an almost continuous rapid. A good canoeman must be quick of eye, strong of arm, and of unerring judgment on these waters. Long light poles shod with an iron point are used almost entirely to force the canoes up the rapids. Upon the man at the bow devolves the duty of guiding the canoe in and out

POOL ON THE ST. ANNE.

among the boulders, around which the waters madly foam. In the heaviest current my two canoemen could hold the canoe stationary for an indefinite time while I fished. Some fine pools here and there gave the men a respite, and ourselves some capital sport. Carrier pool has a name for very large fish, but we failed to break the record of $6\frac{1}{2}$ lbs., but we fished it in mid-day under a bright sun. The Parmachenee Belle appeared to be the most killing fly. At the forks of the Tourilli River another fine pool tempted us, but there was something radically wrong, and nothing larger than $1\frac{1}{2}$ lbs. rewarded our skill. The day, however, was very bright, the water low and very clear, and trout any way are erratic, so we consoled ourselves, landed and had a jolly good smoke. Twenty-seven years before, with only one Indian, carrying each our pack, we had made our way laboriously over the mountains from the Jacques Cartier River, and had camped at this very spot on our way to the *pêche à Markham*, some ten miles further up the St. Anne. We made a rude raft of spruce logs to cross the Tourilli. For an hour before sun-down I used it to fish this pool, and if my memory is not treacherous I believe that I took some half dozen fish of from two to five pounds, I might have taken twenty equally large.

About a mile up the Tourilli are the Falls and the pool of the same name in which some very large trout are always to be found.

Our course was still up the St. Anne to the forks of River Caché, but at the four mile rapid the water was too low for our heavily laden canoes, and Palmer and I took the trail on the bank. Capital exercise bush tramping on a blazed trail, by no means a mere mechanical movement of the legs, but a series of gymnastics of much varied novelty ; high jumping, long distance jumping, balancing, walking a slippery log over a deep stream, climbing a perpendicular wall of rock, sliding down a 90° declivity and landing on your feet, pitching somersaults over treacherous roots into nests of raspberry bushes, maintaining an equilibrium on a sharp point of rock over a boiling rapid. For two rather stout middle aged gentlemen somewhat out of training that four mile tramp suppled us up, and gave us our wind for the climb over the mountain trail to Lake Jambon, a half mile into the clouds in very much the same distance, but we had a good rest before the men got up with the canoes.

Palmer said he was feeling better in many ways, but that he had a constant gnawing sensation in his stomach which he couldn't account for and which was rather alarming.

"Well my boy," said I, "those symptons will be much more alarming to our cook within another twenty-four hours." And there, and then, I cut me an alder pole, and with a piece of casting line and a discarded fly, I waded into the river, and caught a half dozen small trout, which I proceeded to toast over our little smudge fire, and Palmer devoured them all, remarking that the more painful symptons had subsided.

There is a most comfortable little log camp at this point of the river with several wire mattresses, and camp outfit.

Lake Jambon is a lovely sheet of water with some six or eight miles of shore line. It is situated almost at the mountain level, and is of immense depth and of such wondrous clearness that I believe a sixpence could be seen at a depth of fifty feet in its waters. .There is a roomy camp here, and a number of good boats.

When the sun dropped low in the west, and the shadows crept out from the shores over the lake, we went a-fishing. Out of the icy cold water rose trout after trout, and such vigorous fighters that a half-pounder seemed endowed with the strength and life of half a dozen ordinary trout. It was almost dark when I hooked my largest fish, and for at least ten minutes it towed us round and round, but I finally landed it, and it only turned the scales at $1\frac{1}{2}$ lbs. Palmer's success was even greater than mine.

The men had built a great camp fire at the water's edge, and before we turned in for the night they treated us to an improvised concert and many stories of hunting and trapping adventures about this section. In the fall and winter the shores of this lake are much resorted to by caribou.

FISHING THROUGH THE ICE.

We remained at the lake for several days, enjoying good sport, and then returned to the St. Anne.

We ran that four mile rapid just for Palmer's benefit,

to stimulate his liver and excite his heart action. I hadn't time to analyze my own sensations. It was all so sudden, and I was too absorbed in wondering how the men were going to avoid the thousand and one great boulders upon which the canoe was rushing to destruction with lightning speed, when—the canoe was suddenly swung into the mouth of a little stream, our mad race was ended.

Sitting before me on a rock was Chas. Forrest, of Hartford, fighting the black flies.

"My dear fellow, how are you, and won't you have a nip," exclaimed that hospitable gentleman all in a breath."

I could only gasp, "Forrest, you better believe it!"

Palmer was speechless when he arrived; it took two nips to revive him, and his first remark was:

"I'm darned!"

Whereupon we assured him that he certainly would be if he made use of such strong language.

"Boys," said he, "I've lived twenty years in the last twenty minutes. Do you notice that I've grown any grayer?"

And we laughed him to scorn!

Our down fishing to the club house was capital and we were about tied.

A joyous night, another pleasant day, and the train bore us back to Quebec.

A TWO POUNDER.

CHAPTER SEVENTH.

LAKES TANTARI AND "BELLE TRUITE."

> " Oh 'tis sweet to feel the plastic
> Rod, with top and butt elastic
> Shoot the line in coils fantastic
> Till, like thistle down, the fly
> Lightly falls upon the water,
> Thirsting for the finny slaughter.
>   As I angle
>   And I dangle
>   Mute and sly."

A hard day's tramp over the mountains from the settlements lies the beautiful Lakes Tantari, and beyond them, in a deep recess of the mountains, nestles Lake *Belle Truite*, which is known of few men, for not even a blazed trail leads to it, and years may pass without a fly being cast upon its waters, but to him who comes is awarded the certainty of battles royal with the hard fighting denizens of its waters.

You slip suddenly from out of the gloom of dense forest upon the shores of Lake Tantari, and spread before you, in the sweet sunshine of afternoon, is as lovely a sheet of water as ever gladdened the eye of angler. In the years gone by my only craft upon its waters was a log raft, which here let me add, is rather a primitive affair, simply three logs about thirteen feet in length, joined together by birch withes to shorter pieces placed crosswise upon it to form the seats, and in the centre a large corseau of bark makes a safe receptable for the fish. I can assure the reader, that these rafts are as well adapted for fly-fishing as any canoe I have ever fished from. Their broad, flat surface affords a secure foothold, and being elevated but a couple of inches above the water, makes an easy landing for the trout. It is propelled with small effort, and if wind favors, a sail made from a blanket materially assists its progress.

Piling the packs in the centre, but retaining my gun by my side for a stray shot at a duck, with which these inland lakes teem in spring and early autumn, we seize our paddles and our united effort quickly lands us at our old camp on the opposite shore. These summer camps are very similar in construction to the winter ones, with the exception of the stockade, which is dispensed with. Charlo gathers together the remnants of our old fire, and soon has the kettle boiling for our tea and some pork *grillades* frying, which throw out an aroma grateful to hungry men. After our meal we light our pipes and throw ourselves down before the fire for that sweet half hour of perfect rest which comes from living in the woods, but mine was destined to be cut short this day by the following enquiry from Charlo :

" Did you ever hear, sir, of *lac à la Belle Truite ?*"

At this unexpected question I roused myself, and sitting up, exclaimed " Heard of *Belle Truite* ? What an idea!" I had dreamed and talked of it the past six months, ever since Etienne had come into Quebec with a corseau of fish, such as had rarely been seen. All inquiries as from whence they had come only elicited the laconic reply, " *Belle Truite,*" and as no one knew anything of *Belle Truite,* no one was much the wiser. As I had visited Etienne's camps last winter and made myself somewhat familiar with his haunts, I felt within myself a glowing ambition to go and discover *Belle Truite*. After a long discussion it was decided we should make the attempt, and start forthwith, and sleep that night at Etienne's first camp, to commence our search from there on the morrow.

We resume our places on the rafts, and passing through the inlet that connects the lakes, we enter the second. Rising abruptly from its shore some hundreds of feet is Caribou Leap, a mountain so named from an event which happened many winters ago. Charlo's father and companion, while hunting, started a caribou far above the lakes. The snow was deep and yielding, and they rapidly gained upon it. The caribou made for the mountain, his pursuers still closely following, and a shot from Charlo's father wounding it, it dashed wildly toward the precipice, and with one bound sprang from its edge and fell lifeless at the foot.

At the entrance to the third lake we disembark, and hauling up our rafts for greater safety against our return, assumed our packs, and picking up the line of blazes, we reach Etienne's first camp at dusk, and were only comfortably domiciled ere the rain came down in torrents. Our fire spits and sputters in it, but burns up fiercely nevertheless. We sit back under the comfortable shelter, and having improvised a checker board and checkers from birch bark, we while away the few hours before it is time to turn in. I slept soundly, lulled by the incessant patter of rain on the bark roof of the camp, and the fatigues of the day's tramp.

The morning broke fair, and we started out to discover the mysterious lake. The bearings are taken and we finally make a bold push, and ere noon I was rewarded by a sight of our Eldorado—a pretty little sheet of water embosomed among the spruce-covered mountains, about two miles from camp. It would scarcely cover twenty acres in all, and its size certainly could be no criterion for that of its trout. In years past a family of beavers had formed a dam across the outlet, flooding the few level acres around it, denuding them of trees and underbrush. The capture of this interesting family and the destruction of the dam caused the subsidence of the waters to their former level. A rich covering of coarse wild grass now affords famous feeding for the caribou, and we found numerous fresh tracks. The beavers have left many evidences of their industry and skill, in cuttings of all sizes, from one to four inches in diameter, and from the length of cordwood down. Their habit is to bring these twigs and billets to their houses, and after devouring the inner rind or bark, to cast them adrift.

Charlo selects an old dry sound spruce for our raft. Late in the afternoon we launch our craft on the lake, and set out on a voyage of discovery. I splice my rod, and attaching my most tempting flies to my casting line, Charlo paddles towards some lily pads that show themselves in the centre of the lake. As we near them I cast, and scarce had my fly touched the water when rushing upwards with open mouth, a huge trout seizes it, a twist of my hand and I feel that it is secured. Two dozen trout, averaging two pounds in weight, rewarded my skill and fully sustained the name of this little mountain gem. Never before, as a fisherman, had I enjoyed such sport, and it was long after dark before I thought of returning to camp.

It is a difficult thing to pass through a forest at night. It is particularly so where you are obliged to cross numerous windfalls. You walk ten feet on some fallen monarch and are surprised when it comes to an unexpected termination and you are launched into space. Our experience that night returning to camp was, to put it mildly, rough. Rent clothes, scratched hands and faces bore full evidence of it. A good supper and companion pipe put us in good humor and these annoyances are forgotten.

This camp is Etienne's headquarters for balsam gathering, and his implements and ladders are carefully laid beside the stockade. The process of gathering it is quite simple. A small can, the shape of a tin tea-pot, is used to prick the blister filled with the gum with which the balsam trees are covered at certain seasons. Large quantities are thus collected, the market price of which is some ten shillings per gallon. Its healing qualities are well-known.

Upon our return to Tantari we decide to spend the night on the island and enjoy one evening's fishing off the point, which proves to be good. I rose some large trout. It was almost dark when we reached the site of what should have been a camp, but no camp could be found and we ruefully surveyed the prospect of having to build one. No time was to be lost, and setting Charlo to work to peel bark and break balsam branches for the bed, I cut what wood we required for the night, and starting a fire, by its light we finished building our camp, laid our bed and prepared the meal, and not a moment too soon. The dark lowering clouds that had been gathering during the day now opened their floodgates. The thunder and lightning seemed fairly to rend the mountains, and the wind shrieked through the pines. No fire could live long with such a torrent pouring upon it, and it finally went out, leaving us in total darkness and increasing our discomfort. Our camp, hastily put up, was not free from flaws and cracks, through which the water trickled down, now on our backs, heads and legs. Charlo in his haste, in peeling the bark, had split it in a number of places. We lighted our pipes and silently smoked, looking out upon the elements at war, and taking what little comfort was left us. The morning dawned and the storm having ceased, we crawled out from our uncomfortable berth stiff and chilled through to the bone. Having patched up our raft we pulled out to some lily pads in the middle of the lake. They were on a shallow bank some hundred yards in circumference, and at dawn and evening fairly alive with the leaping fish feeding on the large yellow moth or fly that is so abundant on these lakes at certain seasons. The fish take the imitation with avidity. Our showing that morning was five or six dozen beauties.

While following the shore on my return to camp I started out a flock of young unfledged ducklings and

CARIBOU HUNTERS' CAMP NEAR TANTARI.

an exciting chase ensued. Using their little wings as paddles, they soon distanced me, and took refuge among some drift wood. I determined to possess myself of one if possible, and I redoubled my efforts to affect a capture. I chased them finally into a corner, and quietly chuckled as I thought how I had entrapped them. I carefully approached, and stooping down to pick one out, when down they went under my raft, coming up some twenty feet distant. I was totally unprepared for this early evidence of duck learning, but recovered myself and started again in hot pursuit, but was finally obliged to give it up from sheer exhaustion. The old mother duck in the meantime had been swimming around me in a great state of excitement, frequently coming within reach of my pole. Happy over the escape of her young progeny, she exultantly swam off with them to some more secure retreat.

On my last visit to these lakes, while quietly fishing off the island in the third lake in company with Mr. Neilson, two stately moose came crashing through the underbrush down to the lake, and, walking in, slaked their thirst and disported themselves in the water to relieve themselves of the flies, which torment them terribly in summer, and to feed upon the water lilies. To our astonishment they appeared quite indifferent to our presence, and remained for some time, giving us ample opportunity to admire their great size.

We fished off the spring that evening for large trout and captured several after a hard and desperate fight. I found though that the fish were beginning to gather, even this early, for spawning, and were not in as good condition as earlier in the season. In one spawning place I counted thousands, but we contended ourselves with taking only those which still remained near the lily pads.

An amusing incident occurred here last season to my friend Dr. W., of Staton Island. He is a tall, long-legged fellow, and it is proverbial among his friends that these same legs are a source of no small amount of misery to him. He either has no control over them, or they over him. We were each out on our raft early one morning, and having an exciting time among the trout, which rose greedily to our flies. I had struck a large fish, which was giving me some trouble, as he proved sulky and obstinate. All my energies were devoted towards making a successful landing, when a loud splash! splash! about a hundred yards behind me in the direction of the Dr. admonished me that something was up. "Ah! ha!" I mentally ejaculated, "the Dr. has hooked the big fish." A succession of splashes here followed, and fearful lest the Dr. should lose his fish, and intent upon my own, I yelled out to him without turning my head, "Play it, Dr., play it, or you will lose it." No answer was vouchsafed this, and having by this time landed my own fish, I turned enviously to the Dr. and took in the situation at a glance. It was the Dr. himself who was creating all this commotion, in his vain endeavors to pull himself on the raft, but each effort only resulting in a fresh splash. The thing was so absurb that I simply roared. As soon as I could command my risibles I went to his assistance. Hat, seat, fish, rod, corseau, and trout, all floating about promiscuously! Collecting what we could, we made for camp, and starting a fire the Dr. divested himself of his outer garments and hung them up before it to dry. This was all very well until the flies, scenting him out as legitimate prey, made such an onslaught that the Dr., with a howl of pain, made for the lake at a 1-40 rate, never once stopping until he had submerged himself to the neck in the water, and there remained disporting himself until his clothes were dry. His account of the accident was, he had hooked a fish, but in some unaccountable manner, he had tripped and gone in headforemost.

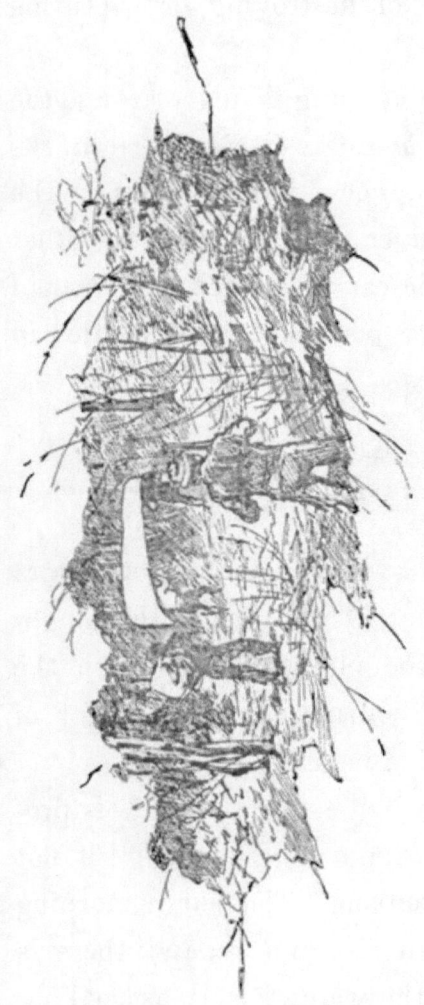

We spent a night at St. Michel Lake. No take. A peculiarity of this lake is that only once or twice in a season will the trout take a fly, and then such sport! On our way along the base of the mountains, on the Jacques Cartier, we saw the ravages made by a party of bears the night previous in an oat field. Not a spear left standing. What was not eaten was trampled and rolled down as flat as a pancake. Their depredations upon the crops of the settlers are sometimes enormous, and yet no systematized method of destroying or capturing them is resorted to.

The last ray of sunshine hung lovingly around the summits of the eastern mountains that close in the valley when wearily we launched our canoe upon the swift, dark waters of the river, and paddled to the other shore, where stood our little camp of a departed year of fragant memories. We are just comfortably settled in our bark wigwam when:

> " Night draws her sable curtain round
> And pins it with a star "

The warmth of our good log fire, the narcotic odors of the balsams, the murmur of the river and the soughing of the wind through the pines, together with the fatigue of the long day's journey, invite a night of refreshing and undisturbed slumber.

Early fishing in these high northern rivers is productive of nothing but discomfort to the angler, if not worse—an attack of rheumatism. The early morning air is too cold for the fish to rise to a fly, and there is always a heavy mist over the water that is as soaking as a Scotch rain. We therefore leisurely prepare ourselves for the day's work. Our little craft dances

A SUMMER CAMP.

merrily in the current and tugs impatiently at her rope to be off on her mad career down the foaming rapids

Charlo takes the helm, with anchor and rope close at his hand to drop when I give the word. We run the first few rapids without stopping, as from past knowledge of the river we know them to be barren of fish, but a perpendicular blue clay bank directly ahead points out first stop. About midway down the rapid, anchor is cast out; there is a sudden tug, a straining to be free, a slight drag and the canoe brings up just where it admits of a good cast into the back current, foam-covered and dark from the depth of the water. A few fine fish are taken, and as the rises are then few, we again proceed. We cover nine miles of the river this day, confining our fishing to those pools and rapids that contained the large fish. On arrival at our destination the weight and score of our fish are duly recorded, which if given would startle the Eastern angler into making, perhaps, a resolve never to again wet a line in other waters.

Lakes Tantari and *Belle Truite* are now the property of Frank Ross, Esq., of Quebec. His son, who is an enthusiastic angler, has built a beautiful little camp on the shores of the former lake, where he spends many happy days. I beg leave here to acknowledge my indebtedness to his kindness, which has enabled me many times to revisit these scenes of long ago, and again to enjoy the pleasure of fishing their waters.

VIEW ON JACQUES CARTIER RIVER NEAR BAYARD'S.

CHAPTER EIGHTH.

THE LAURENTIDES NATIONAL PARK.

" And through its midst there ran a crystal flood
With many a murmering song and elfin shout,
In whose clear pools the crimson spotted trout
Would turn his tawny side to sun and sky,
Or sparkling upwards catch the summer fly."

The Laurentides National Park in the Province of Quebec is the largest forest and game preserve in the world. By the act of the Provincial Legislature creating it, some 2,500 square miles of the public domain was set aside for this purpose, and proper laws for its government were adopted. A committee of the Executive Council recommended that the general management of the Park should be vested in the Hon. Commissioner of Crown Lands, and the Superintendent, and such other officers as the Hon. Commissioner may appoint to carry out the intention of the Legislative Act.

The Park is the result of the direct and unceasing efforts of the present Minister of Crown Lands, the Hon. E. J. Flynn. His name is now forever linked with one of the wisest and most beneficient measures ever passed by a legislative body. It means the preservation of the great forests on the water sheds of some of the most important rivers in the Province. The bearing of this upon the future water supply to these rivers, and upon the rainfall, is now too well understood to require further explanation. The protection to fish and game, which is incidental to the main object, is of sufficient importance, however, to receive the careful attention that it deserves, and to futurity is conserved a vast breeding ground for the fish that now swarm its waters, the game that haunts its forests.

The southerly boundary of the Park reaches down to within twenty-five miles of the city of Quebec at some points; that to the north is the Chicoutimi *Grande Ligne*; to the west the river Batiscan and the Lake St. John R.R., to which I have before alluded ; to the east the river Saguenay and the St. Urbain road. The more precise boundaries will be found in the appendix, as well as text of the act creating the Park.

The more important rivers taking their source within the Park, and flowing through it, are the Jacques

Cartier, St. Anne, Tourilli, Metabetchouan, Upikauba, Boisvert, Mars, Murray, Montmorenci, and their tributaries, also some of the larger tributaries of the Batiscan.

The great divide, from which flow waters to the four cardinal points of the compass, is literally peppered

with lakes, big and little. In one expedition to this country, on snowshoes many years ago, in eleven days journeying we were never off a lake more than twenty minutes. This will give the reader some idea of the immense number which dot the surface of this plateau. Great Lake Jacques Cartier, the source of the river which bears its name, has a shore line of some twenty-five miles, and is justly celebrated for the abundance and size of its trout. I shall have occasion further on to say more of this lake, as well as of Snow Lake, the head of the Montmorenci River, another famous sheet of water. To the west a few miles from Lake Jacques Cartier is Lake Noah.

Lake *des Roches, Vert,* Long, *à Noël, à la Coupe* Fraser, *à Regis, à l'Epaule* all discharge into the Jacques Cartier River, and are easily accessible by the colonization road from Quebec to Lake St. John.

Why attempt to further name the lakes in this section, it would only confuse the reader, and the subject is far too vast for the scope of a chapter. I would refer those who seek for more detailed information in this direction to a little pamphlet recently published in Quebec under the auspices of the Department of Crown Lands entitled, "Our Rivers and Lakes". The south-west, west, north-west, and north edges of the Park have been leased to angling Clubs, and this is a wise measure for the greater protection of the fish and game within the Park limits. These organizations are all directly interested in the increase of fish and game, and jealous guardians of their own leaseholds. It has drawn a cordon of keen watchfulness around the Park, and poaching, or killing game out of season, is rendered almost impossible without instant detection.

The whole of the unleased territory within the Park, some 1500 or 1600 square miles, is to be thrown open to the American and Canadian angler-sportsman upon conditions that every true lover of sport will be only too ready to subscribe to. At present only one section is readily accessible, but as this is to be the highway into the greater domain, and as it embraces some of the best fishing waters, and caribou country, I shall describe it more fully, with suggestions to intending visitors.

The last house on the Jacques Cartier River is Bayard's, a famous little resort for those of the angling fraternity who have been initiated into the comfort and good fare provided by mine hostess, Madame Bayard, and the exceptionally fine fishing in the river hard by. Both are destined to become more widely known in the near future. The Bayards are already adding a wing to their house to provide more ample accommodation. It is twenty-seven miles from Quebec over a fairly good road, and may be reached in a four and a half hour's drive.

Mr. Geo. Colvin, the guardian of that section of the Park known as the Jacques Cartier Basin, resides here, and under his superintendence parties going into the Park can be supplied with guides, canoes, and tents. I know the guides on this upper section of the river and they are all capital river men and thoroughly familiar with the country, trails, and lakes.

The Jacques Cartier is canoeable to the *Grand Portage*, after which it becomes too turbulent, broken by falls and heavy rapids. To this point, however, there are numbers of famous pools from which trout of seven lbs. and over are not infrequently taken. At the mouth of the Santoriski River, and for some distance up that stream, trout are particularly abundant and of good size, and this statement applies as well to the River *à l'Epaule*, both tributaries of the Jacques Cartier. The scenery is magnificently wild, the mountains broken into every conceivable form, a great chaotic upheaval, through which the river winds its noisy, fretful course.

With Bayard's as headquarters, trips may be made either up down the river, with as much or as little camping as the angler cares for.

To him who seeks the wilderness "far from the madding crowd", and prefers the shelter of his little

WINTER SCENE ON COLONIZATION ROAD.

tent or bark lean-to, with the bush and the waters as his foraging ground, a trip to Grand Lake Jacques Cartier will afford a variety of experiences and adventure, and the record breaking big brook trout may be lured by his fly and fall a victim to his skill. Monstrous fish lurk in these waters. A nine pounder has already been placed in the scales, but better than this may be expected.

The long disused colonization road from Quebec to Lake St. John passes close to Lake Jacques Cartier, which is distant about thirty miles from Bayard's. An effort will be made to have this road re-opened for the passage of buckboards this season, and canoes and boats placed permanently upon the lake, besides a substantial log camp at the discharge.

John Burroughs, than whom no name is so familiar to American readers, as the author of " Wake Robin ", " Winter Sunshine ", and other works of one of the most observant of field naturalists, visited Lake Jacques Cartier some years ago, and most charmingly recorded his adventures in the pages of the Century Magazine. Mr. Burroughs very kindly consented to my making some extracts from his article to conclude this chapter :

" About four o'clock we passed another small lake, and in a few moments more drew up at the bridge over the Jacques Cartier River, and our forty-mile ride was finished. There was a stable here that had been used by the road-builders, and was now used by the teams that hauled in their supplies. This would do for the horse: a snug log shanty built by an old trapper and hunter for use in the winter, a hundred yards below the bridge, amid the spruces on the bank of the river, when rebedded and refurnished would do for us. The river at this point was a swift black stream from thirty to forty feet wide, with a strength and a bound like a moose. It was not shrunken and emaciated like similar streams in a cleared country, but full, copious and strong. Indeed, one can hardly realize how the lesser watercourses have suffered by the denuding of the forest covering until he goes into the primitive woods and sees how full and athletic they are there. They are literally well fed and their measure of life is full.

"Three miles above our camp was Great Lake Jacques Cartier, the source of the river, a sheet of water nine miles long and from one to three miles wide; fifty rods below was Little Lake Jacques Cartier, an irregular body about two miles across. Stretching away on every hand, bristling on the mountains and darkling in the valleys was the illimitable spruce woods. The moss in them covered the ground nearly knee deep, and lay like newly fallen snow, hiding rocks and logs, filling depressions, and muffling the foot. When it was dry one could find a most deligthful couch anywhere.

"It was a dull rainy day; the fog rested low upon the mountains, and the time hung heavily upon our hands. About three o'clock the rain slackened and we emerged from our den, Joe going to look after his horse, which had eaten but little since coming into the woods, so disturbed was the poor creature by the loneliness, and the black-flies; I to make preparations for dinner, while my companion lazily took his rod and stepped to the edge of the big pool in front of camp. At the first introductory cast, and when his fly was not fifteen feet from him upon the water, there was a lunge and a strike, and apparently the fisherman had hooked a boulder. I was standing a few yards engaged in washing out the coffee pot, when I heard him call out:

"'I have got him now!'

"'Yes; I see you have,' said I, noticing his bending pole and moveless line; 'when I am through, I will help you to get loose.'

"'No; but I am not joking,' said he; 'I have got a big fish.'

"I looked up again, but saw no reason to change my impression, and kept on with my work. It is proper to say that my companion was a novice at fly-fishing, he never having cast a fly till upon this trip.

"Again he called out to me, but deceived by his coolness and his unchanged tones, and by the lethargy of the fish, I gave little heed. I knew very well that if I had struck a fish that held me down in that way I should have been going through a regular war dance on that circle of boulder tops, and should have scared the game into activity, if the hook had failed to wake him up. But as the farce continued, I drew near.

"'Does that look like a stone or a log?' said my friend, pointing to his quivering line, slowly cutting the current up toward the center of the pool.

"'My skepticism vanished in an instant and I could hardly keep my place on the top of the rock.

"'I can feel him breathe,' said the now warming fisherman; 'just feel of that pole?'

"The fish yielded more and more to the relentless strain, till in about fifteen minutes from the time he was struck he came to the surface, then made a little whirlpool when he disappeared again. But presently he was up a second time lashing the water into foam as the angler led him toward the rock upon which I was perched, net in hand. As I reached toward him, down he went again, and taking another circle of the pool, came up still more exhausted, when between his paroxysms I carefully run the net over him and lifted him ashore, amid, it is needless to say, the wildest enthusiasm of the spectators. The congratulatory laughter of the loons down on the lake showed how even the outsiders sympathized. Much larger trout have been taken in these waters, and in others, but this fish would have swallowed any that we had ever before caught."

"What does he weigh?" was the natural enquiry of each; and we took turns "hefting" him. But gravity was less potent to us just then than usual, and the fish seemed astonishingly light.

"Four pounds, we said; but Joe said more. So we improvised a scale: a long strip of board was balanced across a stick, and our groceries served as weights. A four-pound package of sugar kicked the beam quickly ; a pound of coffee was added ; still it went up; then a pound of tea, and still the fish had a little the better of it. But we called it six pounds, not to drive too hard a bargain with fortune, and were more than satisfied. Such a beautiful creature ! marked in every respect like a trout of six inches. We feasted our eyes upon him for half an hour.

"This success gave an impetus to our sport that carried us through the rest of the week finely. We had demonstrated that there were big trout here and that they would rise to a fly. Henceforth big fish were looked to as a possible result of every excursion. To me, especially the desire at least to match my companion was keen and constant. We built a raft of logs and upon it I floated out upon the lake, whipping its waters right and left, morning, noon, and night. Many fine trout came to my hand and were released because they did not fill the bill."

"One afternoon quite unexpectedly I struck my big fish in the head of the lake. I was first advised of his approach by two or three trout jumping clear from the water to get out of his lordship's way. The water was not deep just there, and he swam so near the surface that his enormous back cut through. With a swirl he swept my fly under and turned. My hook was too near home and my rod too near a perpendicular to strike well. More than that my presence of mind came near being unhorsed by the sudden apparition of the fish. If I could have had a moment's notice, or if I had not seen the monster, I should have fared better, and the fish worse. I struck, but not with enough decision, and before I could reel up, my empty hook came back. The trout had carried it in his jaws till the fraud was detected, and then spat it out. He came a second time and made a grand commotion in the water, but not in my nerves, for I was ready then, but failed to take the fly and so to get his weight and beauty in these pages. As my luck failed me at the last, I will place my loss at the full extent of the law, and claim that nothing less than a ten pounder was spirited away from my hand that day.

"We made an excursion to Great Lake Jacques Cartier, poling up from the lesser lake in the rude box boat, and presently saw the arms of the wilderness opened and the long deep blue expanse in their embrace. We rested and bathed, and gladdened our eyes with the singularly beautiful prospect. The shadows of summer clouds were slowly creeping up and down the sides of the mountains that hemmed it in. On the far eastern shore near the head, banks of what was doubtless white sand, shone dimly in the sun, and the illusion that there was a town nestled there haunted my mind constantly. It was like a section of the Hudson below the Highlands, except that these waters were bluer and colder, and these shores darker than even those Hendrik first looked upon; but surely, one felt, a steamer will round that point presently, or a sail drift into view! We paddled a mile or more up the east shore, and then across to the west, and found such pleasure in simply gazing upon the scene that our rods were quite neglected. We did some casting after awhile, but no fish of any consequence rose till we were near the outlet again, when they responded so freely that the 'disgust of trout' was soon upon us."

The Department of Crown Lands charges a small fee to sportsmen fishing or hunting within the Park limits, and a permit must be taken out either in person at the Department in Quebec, or by letter to Mr. W.

C. J. Hall, the superintendent, Parliament House, Quebec, who will supply all necessary information and secure guides and canoes if wanted.

The following is a copy of a report of a Committee of the Honorable the Executive Council, dated the 15th January, approved by the Lieutenant-Governor on the 16th January, 1896 :—

No. 10. *Concerning the regulations for the management, control and care of the Laurentides National Park.*

The Honorable the Commissioner of Crown Lands, in a report dated the fifteenth of January instant, (1896), sets forth : that in virtue of clause 6 (and subsections of same) of chap. 22 of 58 Vict., establishing said park, it is desirable that regulations be drawn up and adopted for the purposes specified.

In consequence the Honorable Commissioner of Crown Lands recommends that the following constitute said regulations, viz :

1o. The general management shall be vested in the Commissioner of Crown Lands and the Superintendent, together with such officers as the Commissioner may appoint, shall, under his directions, supervise, manage, control and care for said park, with full power to carry out and enforce the following provisions and rules, as well as any other portions of said Act not herein dealt with.

a. The preservation and care of the water courses, lakes, etc., and the forests, lands, and minerals.

b. The prevention and extinction of forest fires.

c. The protection of fish and game of all kinds, and the destruction of obnoxious animals and birds.

d. The manner of dealing with trespassers, the confiscation or destruction of fire-arms, explosives, traps, nets, fishing tackle, or any other contrivances for hunting, fishing or trapping of whatsoever nature or description.

e. The issuing of licenses for hotels, shops or houses for accommodation of visitors.

f. The issuing of licenses to cut timber, or to remove any forest products.

g. The issuing of prospecting licenses and the working and development of mines.

h. The leasing of lands for houses, etc., for the facilities of visitors and tourists.

1. The adjustment of any special cases not herein provided for.

2o. The Commissioner will define the duties of the Superintendent and other necessary officers, and regulate the remuneration to be granted each.

3o. That all visitors to the Park do comply with the provisions of the Act establishing same, and also these regulations.

4o. That a register be kept of names and addresses of all persons visiting the Park.

5o. That no mutilation or destruction of any standing growing timber be permitted beyond what is absolutely necessary for the purposes of camping.

6o. That all camp fires be carefully guarded and extinguished before leaving the spot, and that all provisions of the Fire Act be strictly observed.

7o. That the only manner of taking fish permissible in the waters of the Park be that known as fly-fishing ; that fish taken in any other manner be held to have been taken illegally.

8o. That the trapping of fur bearing animals in the Park be strictly prohibited.

9o. That the carrying and use of fire-arms by

sportsmen and tourists during close seasons for game be prohibited.

10o. That the Park guardians be vested with all powers exercised by forest-rangers, fire-rangers, and fish and game overseers, in addition to the powers exercised by them as park guardians.

11o. That a stated tariff of charges for hunting or fishing, or both, be adopted by the Commissioner of Crown Lands, according to locality.

Certified,

(Signed)   GUSTAVE GRENIER, C.E.C.

AN EVENING'S CATCH IN LAKE EDWARD.

CHAPTER NINTH.

LAKE EDWARD.

" A white tent pitched by a glassy lake,
  Well under a shady tree,
  Or by rippling rills from the grand old hills,
  Is the summer home for me."

My last visit to Lake Edward, or by its more picturesque name of *Lac des Grandes Isles*, was made by railroad. In the stately luxury of a palace car I was whirled there in a less number of hours than it had taken me days to make the same journey twenty years ago. I still recall the eleven long days of tramp, tramp on snowshoes over mountains and across rivers and many lakes, about as the crow flies, until we finally camped on the shore of this, the most beautiful of all the lakes in the Province of Quebec, and here we fished and hunted the caribou, and were happy for many days, for we reigned alone over a vast solitude. With no other shelter than our little V tent, its bed of balsam branches, and our tiny sheet iron stove, we set the cold at defiance, and we lived royally on trout, caribou, partridges and hares, with pea-soup, pan-bread and strong tea. I who had left New York a month before an invalid had now grown strong of limb, fierce of appetite, and hateful of that busy outside world. The charm of the lake held us until I had explored its shores, and visited many of the little isles that crowd its waters.

As youth is the period of adventure, so middle age loves ease, and as I lay back in my easy chair and smoke my Havanna, I dream over the incidents of that long ago journey, the scenes of which again rapidly pass before my eyes from the car windows, but the snow and ice of arctic winter have given place to joyous verdant June, and the rivers and lakes are instinct with the open life of summer days. The great unbroken wilderness is still here, the forest reaching down in the vain endeavor to cover the invasion of man's restless energy into nature's sacred haunts.

Along the Batiscan River, beside which the train runs for many miles, the mountains drop abruptly to its shores, and its turbulent waters drown the noise of passing train. The locomotive whistles, a tiny white tent is seen nestling in a grove on a point, two anglers in a canoe wave a return salute with several great trout held at arms length, a bundle is thrown from the car, and on the train rushes, ever anxious seemingly to escape from the wilderness of which it is no part, with no point of sympathy, but always plunging deeper and deeper into it. Panting with the exertions of the last two hours, the locomotive brings the train to a rest at Lake Edward, and dinner at Baker's cosy little hotel is announced. A half dozen log houses, and a small repair shop constitute the entire settlement on the shores of the lake, an inconspicuous blot in the great wall of forest and hills that extend around a hundred miles of its shore line.

The fishing in the lake is free to all who come, and were they to come in companies, battalions, a regiment of anglers even, there would be ample room for them all, an island perhaps for each man and its surrounding water, and every one of them would be certain to have good fishing, at times, for even in this overteeming with trout lake there are days when the most tempting fly, the liveliest angle, the silveriest minnow will fail to coax a trout from out the depths, but they are not many.

The lake is yet little resorted to. The Quebec

angler prefers his club and its congenial companionship, and the American is still unfamiliar with the wonderfully good fishing in these Canadian waters, and their accessibility. Leaving New York or Boston for Quebec via the Quebec Central R.R., one may reach Lake Edward within forty-eight hours and step out of the palace car into a boat on the lake. Just think of it, dropped from a palace car in the very heart of the wilderness fairly teeming with game, at the edge of a lake which has no equal on this continent for the quantity, size and beauty of its trout, and which in itself alone is possessed of a greater charm of varied picturesqueness than any other body of water in all our lake region. It is perhaps some twenty miles long, but of such irregular and crooked shore lines, and so filled with high-peaked, heavily wooded islands, both large and small, as to form a labyrinthian maze of waterways that extend its length to unknown distances, and prove most confusing to the uninitiated canoeist, who easily loses his course amid the confusion of channels, with his mind absorbed with the exquisite loveliness of his surroundings. He may not expect to know this lake from one visit or from many. Its elusiveness astonishes one, new waters, new islands, are ever opening before you, and you fish, well almost anywhere that fancy prompts, for one thing you soon learn about this lake is that trout are everywhere found. In time you grow cunning and seek for spots wherein the great trout lurk alone, and nothing short of 5 lbs. satisfies your ambition, or is worthy of mention at the evening camp fire, unless it be a brace of four pounders successfully landed on leader and tail fly.

Birkett Clarke, better known as Kit Clarke, the author of "Where the Trout Hide," was among the first of American anglers to visit Lake Edward, and so enamored was he of its many charms that he leased *Isle de Paradis*, not far from the discharge, and formed the Paradise Fin and Feather Club, which numbers among its members President Cleveland, Judge Henry Gildersleeve, Dr. Duncan, J. C. Davis, Henry C. Miner, Dr. E. Lewis, Ex-Mayor Grant, of New York, and others Jovial parties gather at their comfortable camp every year to fish, and be boys again in light heartedness.

The Press Club of Quebec also makes it rendezvous here, and the knights of the quill are no less expert with the rod, while their fish stories prove them past masters of their craft.

Truth compels the statement that in the lake itself in the hot summer months the trout will not rise to the fly, and trolling or still fishing must be resorted to, but with light tackle almost as much sport is obtained, for these Lake Edward trout are the hardest and strongest fighting fish in the world and require considerable skill in handling. In the inlets and the discharge, however, the trout rise voraciously to a fly throughout the season, but to fish the latter a permit must be obtained from the Orleans Fishing Club of Quebec, the lessees. If the angler cares to rough it for a day or two any of the smaller lakes within half a day's tramp from his camp will afford him unlimited fly fishing, though the trout will be smaller.

I had brought my old guide with me to the lake, as well as my birch canoe and canvas lean-to, three most excellent companions to travel with in the Canadian wilds wherever practicable. It prevents uncertainties, disappointments and much hard feeling, and adds immeasurably to one's comfort, besides being cheaper.

We camped far down the lake towards the close of the long June day, but I still had time for an encounter with several large trout, in which I came out triumphant. Flushed with victory, we built a great camp fire near the shore, as a beacon to guide some friends from opposite isle, and for hospitable warmth of welcome to our lakeside retreat.

For the week the world had been dead to them, and already they showed signs of relapsing into complete barbarism. They were an unkempt, unshaven, ragged trio of Bohemians, and their faces bore the marks of fierce battles with the black flies, so that I scarce recognized them, but they were in high spirits and declared that for every black fly bite they could show a trout slain—blood for blood, and they were getting inoculated, and would like to settle their worldly affairs and spend the rest of their earthly existence here, that their disembodied spirits could haunt the same scenes. So they prattled on in the joyousness of men who had lived in the light of another and simpler life, the great out-door of Nature in high altitudes, high latitudes.

My camp fire blazed and crackled right merrily,

lighting up the sombre forest, sending dancing shadows and sparks far up the tree tops, and shooting rays to distant isle. The water lapped the beach in gentle cadence to the soft soughing of summer night wind through the spruce. In the dome of the North flashed the cold light of the Aurora, and from distant hillside came the faint hoot of owl.

A camp fire begets cheerful rumination, and from that to story telling, if there be listeners.

"Boys," said I, (why is it we are always boys in the bush?) "did any of you ever hear of a trout smoking?"

Oh! come off Scribbler, we are ready to swallow almost anything up here, even home-made whisky *blanc*, but don't, please don't, ask us to swallow any yarn of that kind.

"But," said I, "listen and judge then for yourselves."

My friend, F—k H—y, is one of the greatest anglers in Quebec. In the intervals between taking in fire premiums and settling losses he goes-a-fishing, and takes in trout. One Saturday he was on the Stadacona Club lakes, and although the day was lowering with a light wind and a drizzle, he whipped the water in vain. Still-fishing it was the same, trolling was no better. Every well known spot was tried, and still no luck.

Turning to his canoeman, he said, " up anchor and we will go back to camp," and to emphasize his complete disgust at so unusual a condition of affairs he tossed a half smoked and still lighted cigar well out into the lake. No sooner had it touched the water than a monstrous trout came up with a rush and disappeared again with that cigar. H——, in telling the story, always added that it was his last cigar or he would have tried another as a bait, and nothing that his fly book contained resembled a cigar in any wise, but he tried again and again, but he could not get that trout to rise.

His chum P——, reaching camp somewhat later than H——, had the same story to tell of want of success, but added that upon reaching the place where he had last seen H—— fishing, he had taken his little paper match box out of his pocket to get a match and finding it empty, had pitched it overboard, and as it reached the water it was seized by the biggest trout that he had ever seen in the lake.

"That's it," said H, "the very same fish I'—— that took a cigar of mine, and he was looking for a

match in that box of your's old fellow to light it again."

"Ulric, come, sing us a song?"

"Very well, Gentlemen, but I will first tell you the story, so that you will understand the wherefore of it." Cadieux was a voyageur and interpreter famed in the early history of Canada, a man of no small ability in things other than woodcraft. His wife was an Algonquin woman. In the winter he hunted and trapped; in the summer he traded with the Indians. It was in the days when the Iroquois waged ceaseless war on the whites and their Indian allies. Cadieux with his family had wintered on the Ottawa River, at the Little Rock of the High Mountain. In the spring a party of Iroquois appeared. One possible way of escape only remained open to the women and children, to run the boiling rapids, a feat never before attempted, while Cadieux and a companion withdrew the attention of the Iroquois. The signal for the canoes to start was the sound of an engagement. Cadieux placed himself and the young Algonquin in ambush.

As the Iroquois approached Cadieux and his companion opened fire, and then retreated, pursued by the whole band of Indians. The young Algonquin was killed, but Cadieux escaped after incredible exertion, only to find death from starvation at the point of the river from which he had started. As his end approached he scratched a shallow grave, into which he crawled after writing his death song on a piece of birch bark. The song was set to a rude but plaintive air, and is still much in vogue among the voyageurs.

In a full tenor, Ulric sang the song in French, of which I give an English translation of a few verses only:

> "Petit Rocher de la Haute Montagne,
> Je viens finir ici cette campagne !
> Ah ! doux échos entendez mes soupirs ;
> En languissant je vais bientot mourir !"

> Thou Little Rock of the High Hill, attend ;
> Hither I come this last campaign to end !
> Ye echoes soft, give ear unto my sigh ;
> In languishing I speedily shall die.

> Oh, nightingale, go tell my mistress true,
> My little ones I leave them my adieu,
> That I have kept my love and honor free,
> And they henceforth must hope no more of me.

> Here, then, it is the world abandons me—
> But I have held Saviour of man, in thee !
> Most Holy Virgin, do not from me fly !
> Within your arms O suffer me to die !

Nothing more plaintive and touching could be imagined that the last verse, as the rich voice floated over the water—

> Très Sainte Vierge, ah ! m'abandonnez pas,
> Permettez-moi d'mourir entre vos bras !

Several days of rare sport, and cheerful companionship, when silently we folded our tent and stole away in the early dawn so as to catch the train that was to bear us to Lake St. John for a few days with the ouananiche.

Boats, guides and camp outfits may be arranged for at Lake Edward by addressing Mr. J. W. Baker, at that place, who is most assiduous in caring for the welfare of visiting anglers. His little lakeside inn contains a warmth of welcome, and the comfort that proceeds from good house-wifery.

A TRIO OF OUANANICHE.

CHAPTER TENTH.

OUANANICHE FISHING--LAKE ST. JOHN.

"Blue limpid, mighty, restless lakes,
God's mirrors underneath the sky;
Low rimmed in woods and mists, where wakes,
Through mirk and moon, the marsh-bird's cry"

Ouananiche fishing is like the opium habit, once acquired it drags its victim further and further from all the other pleasures of life, and impairs his mental equipoise until he becomes a monomaniac on the subject and loses all sense of responsibility. To indulge this propensity he will face cold, wet, hunger, and flies. His impedimenta of rods and tackle show an utter want of regard for expenditure, and his last cent will go for a ticket to Lake St. John and return. If he fishes from the shore watch his behaviour as the first thrill of a ouananiche hooked passes through his tautened line and rod into the arm, and directly to the brain. An unrestrainable delirium seizes him, the face flushes, the eyes flash, the nostrils dilate and the whole body seems possessed of springs. He rushes wildly up and down the rocks and talks excitedly to himself. His madness communicates itself to the fish, incessant flashes of silver fill the air. Out and across the boiling waters of the rapid the crazed fish wildly dashes in its frantic efforts to escape its implacable enemy, and only when completely exhausted will it allow itself to be reeled in, and fallen upon bodily by the insane angler, who rends the air with exultant shrieks of laughter. If he fishes from his canoe the guides will watch him with assiduous care to prevent him from throwing himself overboard in one of these wild paroxsysms of excitement. He is incurable, and the milder delights of trout fishing palls upon his shattered nerves and diseased brain.

Luckily for the saneness of the race of anglers ouananiche fishing is confined to a limited area of the world's surface. Lake St. John and its tributary rivers are its best known haunts.

The ouananiche is only a degenerate salmon supposed at some remote period or other to have become land-locked. It has diminished in size from its ancestral progenitors of thirty pounds to a fish rarely exceeding five pounds, but retains all the characteristics of form and marking besides the fierce strength and subtle cunning of *salmo salar*. Its habits have been somewhat modified, however, by changed conditions of life, and it not only takes the fly, but at some seasons must be angled for with bait, except in the Grand Discharge, where it takes the fly only. For vigor and gameness size for size it has no compeer. In the rushing waters of the Grand Discharge it becomes an antagonist of no mean ability, requiring skill and dexterity of the highest order to successfully cope with. It fights to the last gasp. For moments the air will be filled with flying fish, succeeded by wild rushes that make the reel sing and the nerves tingle, and this amid the roar and wild confusion of waters. Your light rod will be tested to the last ounce of strain, your line to its utmost tension, and you are lucky if nothing more collapses other than your nerves, as the net is slipped under the still struggling fish, and your first ouananiche is landed. The seed of madness is now in your veins; a few days more and you are a hopeless victim. While there is still time flee the scene, and take a week among the trout in some adjacent lake or river.

The valley of Lake St. John is of considerable

extent. It is an oasis of rich soil and temperate climate in the heart of a sterile mountain wilderness, an arctic climate. Far removed from the greater world, it has developed a small one within itself. It is a simple civilization rubbing shoulder to shoulder with Indian, fur-trader, and voyageur.

The lake is invariably described as an inland sea in appearance, and it is not entirely inappropriate, for no opposite shore line is anywhere visible, nothing upon which the eye rests but an expanse of the bluest of blue water. Yet the lake is but twenty eight miles long at its greatest length, if a body which is almost circular in form can be said to have a length. It is the receiving reservoir of a great number of rivers, some of them large size, and hundreds of miles in length. They flow into it from the West, North and South. At its easterly extremity are the two discharges divided by Alma Island, and united they form the head of the mighty Saguenay River. The lake is shallow for so large a body, but it rises and falls with the rivers which supply it. In the summer great beaches of rock and sand extend for half a mile or more from high water mark, and at a distance of several miles from the shore the water is only of a depth of three or four feet. Sudden and severe storms sweep over it, and ugly seas arise which even prevent the steamers, which have been built for navigating its waters, from putting out into it. The Indians and voyageurs in their canoes never attempt to cross it, but closely hug the shore.

The geology of the shores of the lake is particularly interesting, and the mere casual looker finds many interesting specimens of corallites such as cary ophilliae, chain coral, madrepores, retepores, millepores, and particularly that corallite so much resembling a bee's hive, and called favosite. Much of the limestone also contains fossil organic remains. Mr. Baddeley, of the Royal Engineers, made a complete geological exploration of the lake as early as 1828, and his interesting monograph forms part of the "Report for Exploring the Saguenay and Lake St. John" published in Quebec in 1829. It was not until 1842 that the lease of the King's Posts to the Hudson Bay Company expired, and several years yet elapsed before the lands around the lake were thrown open to settlers, but the parishes increased slowly owing to the absence of any direct communication with the outer world except by steamer from Chicoutimi, which involved a journey over miles of mountain roads, always in bad condition at the best, and oft'times impassable. In winter they were hopelessly locked in.

For years the people clamored for a railroad, but the undertaking was too great for private enterprise; finally large government subsidies made it feasible, and the Quebec and Lake St. John R. R. became an accomplished fact. Population largely increased, and an era of prosperity dawned upon the settlers. The area of cultivable land, however, is narrowly circumscribed and will soon be exhausted.

At Roberval, on the border of the lake, the enterprising builder of the railroad, a citizen of the United States, has erected an hotel which in size and appointments compares more than favorably with the American summer hotels in the mountains; the cuisine is admirable. The Inland House at the Grand Discharge is an adjunct much resorted to by ouananiche anglers. A beautiful little steamer, the Mistassini, now plies on the lake and connects the two hotels.

A few miles to the west of Roberval is Pointe Bleue, where a Post of the Hudson Bay Co. has been established for a hundred years or more. Near the Post is the Montagnais Reservation, and hither for a couple of months of the summer gather these nomads of the North land to trade their furs, build their birch canoes and enjoy the sunshine of a short plenty. Each family has a small house, which, however, they never occupy, but instead erect their tepees in the yard, using the house simply for storage. They have preserved their native language and customs, and are probably the purest blooded Indians remaining, owing doubtlessly to their limited intercourse with the white man. In August each family sets out for the hunting and trapping grounds far up some river, where they remain until the breaking up of the ice on the rivers in the following spring. Farnham thus described one of these autumn migrations:

"The families that were to 'leave town' were on foot early in the morning, packing up for their long and solitary voyage. As I had discovered no leave-taking on the previous day, I was on the watch for it during the loading of the canoes at the water's edge. The tent was spread on the bottom amidships to protect the bags of flour, rolls of blanket, guns, kettles, traps; there were also rolls of birch bark for roofing the cabin, a roll of baby packed in moss for swathing-clothes and laced up in its straight envelope, and from three to five dogs in each canoe. The only people on the beach, besides the travellers, were half a dozen girls, who squatted on the sand, and surveyed the preparations with considerable indifference."

"'Abroad'! said the man. His wife struck her paddle against the side of the canoe, and dipped her moccassined feet in the water to get rid of the sand, and then climbed over the baggage to her place in the bow. The dogs were thrown in for the fourth time, the children settled among the packs, and he shoved off. They paddled away in silence, the wife kneeling in the bow, the heads of the children and dogs showing above the gunwale, and the man sitting up on the bar at the stern. Their families and their valuables were all intrusted to a frail little craft; their separate routes lay through a wilderness, following the tracks of wild animals; and their last stage may be a fruitless hunt, starvation, and death in a polar night. And yet there was not the wave of a hand from a single soul, nor even a last look at a friendly face."

The Ouiatchouaniche was high and noisy, and foam crested where it pours over the rocks into the lake, and the village of Roberval was locked in silent sleep when we launched my canoe for our long paddle down the lake to the Grand Discharge. I had no mandate, however, to be back in Quebec at any particular date, and preferred this means of reaching our destination rather than by steamer, and we were outfitted like the voyageurs of old, prepared to live upon the country. We ran into the mouth of the Ouiatchouan River and landed for breakfast, and a tramp to the falls a mile inland. I lost my way a dozen times amid the labyrinth of cow paths among the rocks, alders and swamp, but coming suddenly upon the falls, their wild and majestic beauty held me spell bound. From out of the sky dropped a vast volume of amber water lashed in its descent by great projecting rocks into yellow spume, and through the uplifting mists a brilliant rainbow flashed against the dark green mountain side. The great pool into which the water sank eddied and fretted against the flower covered bank, upon which I threw myself to dwell upon the enchanting prospect.

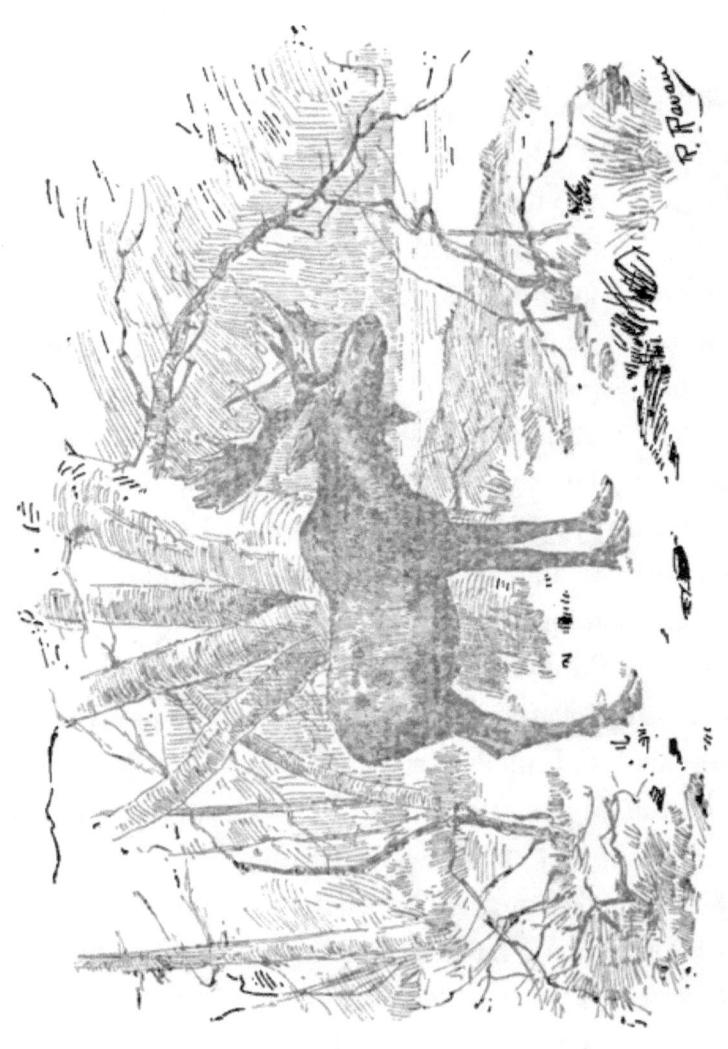

There is a capital bit of ouananiche water between the falls and the mouth of the river, but it is controlled by Frank Ross, Esq., of Quebec, and I was without a permit to fish it.

Lakeward from our canoe the horizon is an expanse of water and sky, but in shore the light and shade of the human life which attached to it robbed it of any loneliness. A continuous row of houses marks the line of road which follows the border of the lake at varying distances. The fields are carpeted in many shades of green. The background of low mountains shows the effect of the devastating fires which have run over them, but they are full of color, and devoid of the sombreness of the spruce clad hills.

We camped at even-tide on a point at the mouth of the Metabetchouan River, not far from an old Hudson Bay Post, but all traces of the yet older Jesuit mission and chapel have disappeared. I wonder if these good fathers in their wildest dreams ever pictured this far away wilderness peopled by those of their own race and faith. They were wonderful explorers these Jesuits, and their geographical knowledge of the interior of the country was more complete than is ours to-day.

The Metabetchouan River takes its source not far from Lake Jacques Cartier. Its upper waters are now under lease to the Philadelphia Fishing and Game Club, of which Mr. Amos R. Little is president. The central portion is controlled by the Metabetchouan Club, of which U. S. Senator Platt, of Connecticut, is president. Some twelve or fifteen miles of the lower part of the river is held by the Amabilish Club, and Mr. E. T. Brewer, of Springfield, Mass., is its president. Right worthily do the members of these clubs uphold the honor of Uncle Sam in Her Majesty's Dominion, as representative citizens, and ardent knights of the rod. The coming of *les Grand Messieurs* is one of the signal financial events in the year among the host of those who benefit from their liberality. This very excess of liberality has lent to every American the reputation, among these simple Canadians of being *bien riche*, and he is worshipped accordingly, and welcomed as the dispenser of all good things.

The following morning we passed the mouth of *la Belle Riviere*, the old canoe route to Chicoutimi on the Saguenay, through Lake Kenogami, and down the Au Sable River, instead of by the Grand Discharge, which necessitates long and heavy carries. At the Little Discharge I found the two canoemen, who were to be my guides through the turbulent waters of the river to the haunts of the ouananiche, in readiness to proceed, a pair of sturdy, hardy-looking fellows, full of self reliant courage, and the most wonderful adepts in piloting their frail craft up and down the treacherous rapids, the swift whirling currents, with only their paddles, stout arms, and unerring judgment. I have forced my way up stiff rapids, I have run miles of rough water, but I should have been as a novice in the mighty currents of the Discharge. I could appreciate to the full, however, the skill and coolness of these intrepid *voyageurs* under all the conditions of their dangerous calling. Yet accidents are of rare occurrence.

In a whirling eddy, out of the *broue*, churned into being by the vast force of the water, and floating in circles, I hooked and landed my first ouananiche with many encouraging words and friendly suggestions from my clever mentors as what was best to do in the exciting moments of the great struggle. I caught many more, and also lost not a few, for this fishing was new to me, and I was fighting a foe whose wiles and strength were unlike anything in my previous experience. I had to unlearn some knowledge and acquire other, but the spirit of these wild waters, the desperate battling of the fish, filled my whole being, and forgetful of civilized training, I became as the primitive man with the fierce love of killing upon me.

At night my camp fire became the scene of another kind of piscatorial contest that tested the resources of the cook, and proved all the game qualities of *salmo salar, variety Sebago,* and the staying powers of four ravenous men, counting the cook. These orgies were followed by pipe, song, and graphically told legends of the dark river.

The days passed quickly until the regretful one of *bon voyage Monsieur, un autre fois!* and **Le Huron** sped away up the lake on the return to Chambord Junction under the strong stroke of paddles.

The land of the ouananiche, its life and struggles are the theme which has engaged the literary leisure for some years past, of an ardent devotee of ouananiche fishing, and shortly, so 'tis said, the angling literature of the world is to be enriched by an exhaustive work on the subject from his pen. The gifted writer, E. T. D. Chambers, of the editorial staff of the Quebec *Chronicle*, is the greatest living authority on the ouananiche, and his forthcoming work will be certain to receive an enthusiastic welcome.

WINTER FISHING.

CHAPTER ELEVENTH.

AN ANGLER'S NOTES.

"If thou wouldst read a lesson that will keep
The heart from fainting, and the soul from sleep,
Go to the woods and hills! No tears
Dim the sweet look that Nature wears."

NATURE'S SUPPLY STORE.

In the northern wilderness, Nature has abundantly provided man with the requisites for a moderate luxury. It is no exaggeration to say, that were an old woodsman placed in the heart of the wilderness and deprived of everything but his clothes, a flint and steel, and a knife, and told to shift for himself, he would in a very short time make himself exceedingly comfortable, leading a regular Crusoe existence in fact, and in time would make his way to the settlements richer in worldly goods that when he started.

From thirst he cannot suffer, as water, pure and undefiled as the dews from heaven, is everywhere abundant, but to allay the cravings of hunger he must speedily devise means. Every little balsam swamp, he knows, abounds with hares and partridges, and without losing any time he sets to work to effect their capture. With the aid of his knife and the abundance of dead brush he constructs a low fence extending several acres across this swamp. At intervals he has left small openings. He next gathers some of the long, tough, pliant roots of the swamp spruce and fashions them into slip-nooses, which he sets at the openings he has left in his fence. His next care is to provide himself with shelter. Yonder yellow birches yield their outer bark readily, and from it a small lean-to is formed, and a fragrant and soft couch is made from the balsam branches. A short search about the camp discovers some Indian tea growing. This makes a very agreeable substitute for the tea of commerce. But how is he going to boil water for tea? exclaims the reader. Nothing easier; the birch bark from which the woodman has constructed his lean-to can be fashioned into vessels that will hold water, and stones heated and dropped into the water bring the latter to boiling point in incredibly short time. Undismayed by his position and certain of a good breakfast in the morning, our woodsman goes supperless to bed. Sure enough, a visit to the snares in the morning discloses several hares and partridges suspended in mid-air. After a hearty meal is partaken of, our friend sets himself to fashion a line from the intestines of one of the hares, and then to make himself a rude hook from a tough splinter of birch wood. As primitive as are these appliances, and with no bait but a piece of partridge meat, he succeeds in landing several dozen small trout from the brawling stream near by that literally teems with fish. Well provisioned now, he packs his provender in a spruce bark *corseau*, and, laying his course by the stream, he jogs off as light hearted as a schoolboy. He knows this stream must fall into a river somewhere, and that river must bring him sooner or later to the settlements.

When after a couple of days he reaches the river he remains camped beside it several days, laying in a store of provisions and constructing himself a canoe of spruce bark to float himself down stream. He searches out a large, clean stemmed tree and denudes it of its bark in one large sheet for some ten or twelve feet from the ground. He then makes a frame of cedar poles that will exactly fit the bark, and the two are lashed firmly together with the spruce roots. Some gum and rosin are next hunted up and applied to the seams at the ends to render the canoe water tight. While by no means as serviceable as a birch canoe, the spruce canoe with care proves an excellent makeshift. We shall now leave our woodsman, conscious that the remainder of his journey will be uneventful.

FOREST BIRDS.

The silence and solitude of the great northern forests is rarely broken by the blithesome song or presence of birds, yet in the trackless wilds of the far interior I have made the acquaintance of several rare and interesting species by habits of close observation. They are an unobtrusive family, as their predilection for the deep forests attests, and not much inclined to court the society of man, though there is one noteworthy exception to this rule, as I shall presently show. So full are they of the immensity and grandeur of these sombre old woods, that it has imparted to them a sober, quiet thoughtfulness, a joyous peal of light-hearted melody being rarely heard—not that they are gloomy or morose, but only earnest, intense, finding life something more precious than an idle holiday to be spent in frivolity. They no doubt also feel a quiet thankfulness in their escape from the manifold dangers that encompass their less thoughtful brethren of the field from the predatory attacks of hawks, crows, reptiles and man. The latter, by the way, ceases to be a foe of the small feathered race as soon as he is beyond the pale of civilization; the former rarely extend their journeyings beyond it.

There is a little dun-colored bird that has a call that sounds precisely like the thud of an axe in a log. The imitation is so exact that I have several times diverged from my course to find out who was encamped near by, to be suddenly recalled to a knowledge of the chopper by hearing the sound repeated in another direction as my shy little feathered friend flew off at my approach. There is still another little inhabitant of the forest, not in good repute, however, with old bushmen, as its presence and short, querulous k-a-t-e is said by them to be followed by a storm. It defies the severest cold of the long arctic winter. It is called the red-bellied nuthatch (*Sitta canadensis*).

The snowy owl—the great northern hunter as it

is aptly named—the barred owl and the cinereous owl are to-day only stragglers into the depths of the forest, adventurous travellers, though their forefathers were dwellers therein. Their change of habitat has been brought about by the greater abundance of food to be procured upon the outskirts of the settlements or the barren lands. The northern hare, upon which the snowy owl and the cinereous largely subsist, has multiplied ten-fold within the boundaries of civilization, as has also the ruffed grouse. The barred owl is said to have the curious habit of burying its body in the soft snow, the large head conspicuous by a pair of bright black eyes only appearing above the surface, forming a grotesque sight.

At rare intervals I have had my camp intruded upon by one or the other of these owls, who, having satisfied its traveller's curiosity, uttered its blood-curdling, sleep-destroying cry, would betake itself again into the quiet shades of night.

Twice in mid-winter I have seen a pair of ravens circling high in air over the frozen lake. At times, uttering their hoarse croaks, they appeared the embodiment of loneliness. What could have tempted them from the sea-coast to the far interior I know not.

The woodpecker family is about the most fully represented one throughout the forest region, the most conspicuous, both for its size and rich markings, being *P. pileatus.* It is by no means common, though widely distributed. The woodpeckers play an important part in nature's economy. By their perforations, in the trunks of dead trees they hasten their decay and fall. Four species winter in Canada, but during the prevalence of severe cold they entirely disappear, a slight thaw, and they are again actively at work. I have been led to think from this that they might hibernate for short periods.

The exception to the shyness of the forest birds is the Canada jay, alias whiskey jack, moose bird, etc. It is about the size of the blue jay, but unlike its congener, its plumage is of a dull, leaden color, and its song a soft continuous warble. I have never camped in the wilderness, winter or summer, that I have not had a visit from a pair of these singular birds. Fearless of man, they would take up their quarters on the nearest twig to the fire and watch their opportunity to steal whatever was left unwatched a moment. Growing bolder each day we remained, they would alight at our feet and scramble and quarrel for the tidbits thrown to them, and otherwise cut up such queer sober antics as to constantly excite my risibles. It is said to breed in midwinter, but if such is the case the male must relieve the female upon the nest, as the germ in the eggs would perish upon the least exposure to the intense cold. I am rather incredulous about this, as I am about the stories that are told concerning its ability to capture fish in the water like a kingfisher.

The aquatics are a numerouly represented family throughout the lake region, where they breed, and in the early fall the angler, while fishing, obtains many a chance to bag a few ducks to add to his bill of fare.

THE RED SQUIRREL.

If there is a sedateness and sobriety on the part of the forest birds, the levity and volubility of this little denizen of the coniferous forests enlivens the general gloom. Summer and winter it is equally cheerful and active. While its favorite haunts are in the deepest recesses and solitudes of the wilderness, it is becoming a frequent visitor and resident of the settlements. The

Indians of the lower provinces have a very pretty little legend about the red squirrel. According to this the squirrel was once upon a time a very large and ferocious animal, much feared by the people, but the good Manitou, desirous of conferring a mark of esteem upon one of the old men of the tribe, asked him what it was he most desired. The reply was, "To have this mighty squirrel made smaller." The Great Spirit at once granted the request, and the old man going forth, spread out his arms and commanded the squirrel to become smaller, and immediately it was reduced to its present size. This is the reason assigned by the natives for its querulousness upon the sight of man, its old enemy.

This little chatterbox is given to migrating occasionally, and if in the course of its journeyings it comes to a lake or a river it takes to the water unhesitatingly and appears as much at home in it as its first cousin the muskrat. In the coniferous woods the red squirrel lays by no provision for the winter, but depends upon the cones to furnish it with a sufficiency to carry it through the long months of snow and ice.

JOTTINGS BY THE WAY.

The elevation of the banks of a river at the foot of a rapid mark the height of that rapid. In the estuaries of rivers and the head of rapids islands are always formed. Deep holes in rivers instead of filling up from the deposits brought down from above by the floods gradually grow deeper. To effect this there must be a strong under-current, during heavy freshets, or whirlpools with a set toward the lower end of the pool. In no other way could they purge themselves. Among ledges of limestone and blue clay in river bottoms large round holes are frequently found. These holes are formed by a hard flint-like spar stone, and the action of the current, which whirls them around and around precisely as the burr stones of a mill revolve.

Snow is dissolved by thawing to one-fortieth part of its bulk, and the process of melting it is so slow and toilsome that it is of the utmost importance in winter to find water near camp. It is always advisable, therefore, to camp beside a lake or a rapid stream. From the former enough water can be collected from the surface of the ice by scraping away the snow. The weight of the latter depresses the ice and causes the water to rise over it, which it also prevents from freezing. All frozen waters must have a breathing place, therefore air-holes are always to be found, or rather avoided, in lakes and rivers. They are necessary, too, for the life of the fish as well.

In summer thunder-storms are of frequent occurrence, and rage with great violence for a short time. They spring out of what was but a few moments before a bright, unclouded sky, but they as quickly disappear, and all nature smiles again. Wind storms are not uncommon that lay waste extensive tracts of country, leveling the mighty forest before them like so many reeds. Such tracks are termed windfalls by the settlers, and are execrated by every one who has occasion to cross them.

Forest Indians always walk intoed for two very good reasons. Were they to walk with the toes turned out they would be constantly tripping amidst the loose roots and the brush, and secondly, the habit of wearing snowshoes enforces the intoe step. It is an imperative law of snowshoeing, to red and white alike, to walk with toes well turned in; an attempted violation of this unwritten code is swiftly followed by a severe punishment—a "header" into four or five feet of snow, from which it is no easy matter to extricate one's-self.

Cattle on a bush farm, where they are much troubled with flies and mosquitoes, soon lose all dread of a fire, and often seek its protection as against their little winged tormentors. Often large smudge fires are burned for them in their pastures. I have seen them rush headlong into it to obtain relief from the venomous attacks of the insects.

Large forest trees much exposed are often split by the extreme action of the frost, which expands their outer fibres more than they can bear. The rent is always accompanied by a loud report like the explosion of a small cannon, and is startling in the extreme in the quiet stillness of night. Rocks are sometimes similarly acted upon where there are seams into which the water percolates and then freezes.

Wherever extensive fires have burned off the coniferous forests an entirely different growth takes place. Birches, poplars, wild cherry, etc., spring at once into luxuriant growth and form a tangled gnarl, through which it is difficult to force a way. Many bush fires are occasioned by the lightning striking some old dry *chicot*.

Trout are not often captured by the fish hawks, for they are about as quick as their feathered foe, and at the first flash they dart away. It is the heavy sluggish fish, such as the suckers, which lie motionless and asleep in the warm, shallow waters, that fall a prey to the keen-eyed hawk. As the capture of such vile fry is no small gain to a stream, the fish hawk must be considered a benefactor to the race of anglers. Suckers consume an immense amount of trout spawn.

People always smile incredulously when the angler relates his ill luck in losing his largest fish, but it is neverthless the case that the very large fish more often escape than find their way into the angler's creel. I have captured some old stagers that from the numerous scars about the mouth showed their frequent acquaintance with the angler's fly.

Rivers upon which much logging is carried on, while they may abound with trout, afford poor fly fishing. The fish are so often disturbed by the drifting logs that they seek the still, deep waters, and feed upon the bottom. Some of the most beautiful rivers in Lower Canada, and famous for large fish, have been almost ruined for fly fishing the past few years from this cause.

Trout when they attain a very large growth, become almost entirely cannabalistic. The better to conceal their nefarious practices, they keep to the deep dark waters of some hole in the stream, sallying forth at night upon their smaller and more helpless brethren. Early in the spring they seek the rapids to cleanse themselves from the parasites that infest them, and they will then rise to the fly, but very rarely at other times.

Feeding and the nature of the water are the two principal causes of the diversity in the coloring of trout, and their form. In very rapid, clear streams the trout are very brilliantly marked, and are lithe and long. In the quiet waters of the lakes the lazy life and abundant food gives them a rotundity of form and duller markings.

Large trout are usually found in couples. Can it be that as they advance in life they permanently mate? Is it simply a platonic affection, the desire for the congenial companionship, the mutual aid and sympathy extended to each other? Who knows?

CHAPTER TWELFTH.

CARIBOU HUNTING.

> "See how the great old forest vies
> With all the glory of the skies,
> In streaks without a name;
> And leagues on leagues of scarlet spires
> And temples lit with crimson fires,
> And palaces of flame!"

Early in September from out of the dome of the North, Jack Frost sets forth as the early herald of coming winter. Jauntily tripping over mountain and table-land, with his magic frozen tipped wand, he gaily touches the maples and birches, and their green livery of summer is instantly changed to the many dazzling hued dress of autumn. The mountain sides fairly blaze with color. He drops in among the ferns and wild flowers that carpet the ground, and all but the gentians, the golden rods and the ragged asters wither at his first approach. With the pines and hemlocks, the spruces and balsams, he has no concern, and they sigh gentle requiems over the departed summer of many fragrant memories. The wild ducks from the farther north fill the lakes and streams, and the lonesome cry of loon in the still night, is replaced by the honk of passing geese high over tree tops. Again the partridge drums upon the fallen tree, while the woods resound with the shrill cries of blue jays.

If the angler will now discard, at times, his rod for trusty rifle, and seek the seclusion of some distant lake for caribou, his quest will not unlikely meet with a reward. Silently his canoe must be paddled around its shores until the day and hour comes when rounding some point, there, in all its beauty, standing in the water, is a buck of noble proportions with mighty antlers. A quick and well directed shot, as he turns to reach the shore, and the proudest moment of your life will be revealed. Your guide will soon disrobe him, preserving the head, which is to adorn your hall. The hindquarters will supply you with most delicious roasts and steaks to vary the diet of pork and trout. You have become an open and avowed admirer of *Rangifer Tarandus* over all of the other deer family, and this will not be your first and last visit into its haunts.

The woodland caribou is more or less numerous

throughout the entire Province of Quebec, but it thrives best in the great forests which cover the mountains and plateaus on the north shore of the St. Lawrence River. It requires room, for with its restless instinct it is ever on the move. However attractive its environment may be, the charm is but temporary before the consuming desire for pastures new. The caribou, which is here to-day, may be a hundred miles away within the next thirty-six hours, and always at home in its every change. I doubt whether the same caribou ever returns to the same spot a second time. Yet the vast numbers which roam this wilderness make an endless procession, but of uncertain movement, without much purpose. It is capable of prodigious and long sustained movement over the roughest country; nothing stays its course if once thoroughly alarmed, and following its trail under such circumstances would be very much like running after an express train.

The nomadic habits of the caribou are among its safeguards against its greatest enemy—man, but nature has abundantly provided it with others to prolong its continuance until long after every other variety of deer has been exterminated. Its shallow hoofs possess an immense area, terminating in sharp edges, while its dew-claws, which are also large, serve a purpose too. Passing over treacherous bog or deep snows, the hoofs and dew-claws are widespread, enabling it to skim lightly over their surface. It walks a fallen tree like a goat and in prodigies of mountain climbing or jumping from a height the caribou might compare with the chamois. No lake or river is too wide for it to swim, and the poorer the country the greater abundance of its favorite food. It revels in the intense cold and deep snows of winter, for its deep thick fine coat of hair amply protects it against all inclemencies of weather, and the long gray moss hanging from fir and spruce, or that which adheres to the bark of the birches upon which they subsist for many months in the year, are the more readily reached from high snow-bank.

A buck caribou will stand about four and a half feet at the fore-shoulder, and will weigh about five hundred pounds. The color is very variable in different animals at all seasons, from the almost perfect white of an old bull in winter to a reddish brown in summer, but no two are ever alike either in markings or in antlers. The latter in general resemble a reindeer's, being somewhat palmated, but of very great uneveness in size and form. The right antler never perfectly matches the left, and one brow antler is sometimes missing, or perhaps both. The cows are also provided with diminutive antlers—unlike all others of the *cervidae*. They are somewhat smaller than the buck, weighing about three hundred pounds. They calve late in May or early June.

The caribou is fond of the companionship of its own kind, and not infrequently droves of ten to fifteen are met with, but oftener three or five. The sense of smell appears highly developed, and upon it, it relies to warn it of approaching danger, to the exclusion almost of sight and hearing. Up wind it may be stalked to within thirty yards, and a dozen shots fired before those remaining are driven off.

It loves the borders of lakes in winter and will spend the greater part of the day in the sunshine on the snow covered ice, the whole herd gambolling about like young lambs, pawing up the snow and slush, prodding and poking each other about, and otherwise comporting themselves in a most ridiculous manner, until the leader, a bull, gives the signal, and the herd falling sedately into line, they slowly march off into the bush in single file like a lot of old cows to pasture.

When lakes and rivers are locked in icy fetters, and all the land and frozen waters are covered with a deep soft carpet of snow, the hardy and intrepid sportsman dons his snowshoes—those matchless snow canoes of winter which lay bare to him many of the hidden secrets of the bush—and their trail will now lead over many miles of mountains, and across rivers, lakes and swamps, as the crow flies, until well within the passing haunts of the caribou. He is prepared to face days of cold and exposure, and if necessary the long arctic night, with no other roof over him save the star-lit vault of heaven, a bed of balsam boughs in the snow, and a big log fire at his feet for warmth, but this only when caught far from camp at the close of the short day after a successful chase may be. I have spent numbers of nights in this manner while following the fresh trail of a herd of caribou, to pick it up on the following morning with the settled knowledge that I should come upon my game upon some lake, or quietly feeding in some swamp. If chance favored and a good first shot is obtained at one of the bulls, another not unlikely becomes a victim.

Building a great fire in the snow, the two caribou are skinned before it, the choice bits are cut out and rolled in the still wet skins, and my Indian and I each shoulder a load to carry back to our main camp. The bucks rarely carry horns in winter and no attention is therefore paid to the heads.

Atkins, one of my guides, once wounded a buck by a long distance shot, but it escaped into the bush with Atkins in hot pursuit on its track. He had not travelled a mile when he observed that the trail of the wounded caribou was joined by that of a *loup cervier*, evidently in as lively chase of the buck as he was himself. Coming out upon a little lake, he was just in time to see the caribou staggering into the bush on the opposite side with the *loup cervier* firmly fastened upon its foreshoulders, and tearing away at its throat with its teeth. Hastening on, he found the caribou fallen and the *loup cervier* gorging itself on the flesh of the still gasping buck. The *loup cervier* was disposed to dispute possession with George, but a well directed bullet ended its career. The lynx or *loup cervier* roams the whole north, and preys principally upon the great northern hare, but it will at times even attack a caribou in the manner just described and bleed it to death while clinging to its back.

There is a profound quiet in the winter woods, but they are by no means destitute of life, as one might otherwise suppose were it not for the tell-tale records in the snow of the most minute track of mouse even. Our snowshoes carry us into the resorts of all the animals which inhabit the wilderness, and if my guide happens to be an Indian no sign is so trivial as to escape his watchful eye, and each tells its story to his experienced knowledge of the sign manual of the bush. A balsam, whose bark has been torn off on one side five or six feet from the ground, shows him that a bear has been there in the spring to suck the fresh run sap, a medicinal draught, and the claw marks indicate its size and age. He calls my attention to some bushes and branches of trees that have been nipped, and says, that two or three moose had passed there in the early fall, and were browsing as they travelled, a bull and two cows "mebbe." If I question the correctness of his interpretation of the signs, he will carefully and logically prove that he has read them aright. A gutter like trail in the snow, as though a log had been hauled along it by some invisible hand, and he informs me that an otter has crossed from one stream to another not more than a couple of hours ago. A wolverine track—the *carcajou* of the Indian, rouses all the savageness of my guide; the despoiler of his traps, the *bête noire* of his winter life, a thieving, cunning rascal who sets him at defiance, and robs him right and left, and the beast will not be caught nor decently allow himself to be shot. The poor Indian's camp even isn't free from the villain's raids while he is absent—and much else of a highly abusive nature. He make the sign of the cross, for he firmly believes the *carcajou* to be the Indian's devil, or evil spirit.

Pointing to a clot of broken snow on the otherwise smooth surface, he says, partridge buried there, cuts a long slender balsam with bushy top, and stealthily advancing, brings the top down with a crash over the spot. There is a confused whirr and struggle, but my Indian has dropped the pole and thrown himself bodily upon the struggling bird, which he soon holds up to my gaze with conscious pride.

He finds signs of beaver about the little lake near

the camp, but there is only one, an old male, and his habitat a hole in the high bank. He will trap him sure.

My little camp is but a small canvas tent well banked at the sides with snow, with sheets of bouleau bark spread over the top to keep in the heat. A diminutive sheet iron stove, that folds up for greater convenience of carrying, and telescopic pipe, keeps us sufficiently warm through the long cold nights. We have carpeted the floor with a great depth of balsam boughs, over which our caribou skins are spread. No more comfortable bed could be devised. A candle, stuck in a split stick, gives us ample light to carry on our light domestic duties, or the odds and ends of repairing to snowshoes and clothes, the cleaning of rifles. By eight o'clock we are in sound slumber, which only the diminishing fire and the increasing cold rouses one of us to pile in more wood, followed by a quiet smoke in the dark. Sometime in the night the candle is again lighted, a caribou steak is fried and eaten, and again sleep is courted.

Shortly before we reached camp on the preceding evening we found what I took to be a single caribou track crossing our old trail, but my Indian said that there were three, that they had travelled a long distance and were not feeding, but they would undoubtedly stop at the little lake on the mountain to sleep, and feed about the shores in the morning.

A look, at peep of day, disclosed it was snowing.

"*Bon*," exclaimed Charlo, "we get em caribou, no fear."

The Indian was right, we stalked those caribou up wind on the lake border to within thirty yards. My shot dropped the buck to his knees, and Charlo finished him with another. The does we allowed to escape, though they circled about their fallen leader for some moments in a most distraught manner, and we might easily have killed them both.

Breaking camp is always a regretful hour, for despite some hardships which we may have undergone, the life possesses a singular fascination, and we become attached to our little mountain home. Toboggans are laden, a last farewell smoke is indulged in, snowshoes are tied, and the homeward trail is taken.

FIRST HOUSE IN QUEBEC.

CHAPTER THIRTEENTH.

Angling Clubs in the Quebec and Lake St. John District.

RIVER OR LAKES.	LESSEES
Saguenay River (Part)	J. G. Aylwin Creighton
Wessoneau	Laurentian Club
Metabetchouan (central part)	Amabelish Club of Springfield, Mass.
" (upper part)	Penn Fishing & G. Club
Tourilli & St. Ann	Tourilli Fish & G. Club
Jeannotte	Orleans Fish & G. Club
Metabetchouan (lower part)	E. Wurtcle
Grand & Little Peribonca	H. J. Beemer
Islands of Lake St. John	H. J. Beemer
Aux Ecorces	Upikauba F. & G. Club
Aux Rats	Press Club
Little Batiscan, &c.	Little Saguenay F& G C
Riviere aux Rognons, etc.	Stadacona F. & G. Club
Des Commissionaires	F. M. Ryder
Long, Des Isles, Vert, etc.	Club Les Laurentides
Najouaoualank	Metabetchouan F.&G.C.
Clair	W. P. Greenough
Kiskisink	Metabetchouan F&G.C.
Des Passes, Batiscan, etc	Triton Fishing Club
Clair	Dr. M. H. Brophy
Kenogami	Rev. W. Barrabé

Extracts from the Game Laws of Quebec Province.

Close season in which it is forbidden:

1.—To hunt, kill or take deer and moose from January 1st to October 1st.

2.—To hunt, kill or take caribou from February 1st to September 1st.

3.—To use dogs for hunting moose, caribou, and deer, but red deer may be so hunted in the counties of Ottawa and Pontiac between the 20th of October, and 1st of November.

4.—To hunt, kill, or take moose and deer while yarding.

5.—To hunt, kill, or take at any time fawns up to the age of one year, or the young of moose or caribou.

6.—No person can, in one season's hunting, kill or take alive more than two moose, three deer, and two caribou.

N.B.—The Commissioner, however, may grant special permit to any person domociled in the Province, on payment of Five Dollars, to hunt, kill, or take alive three additioanal caribou and deer at most, or he may exempt from payment of such fee any *bona fide* settler, or Indian, whose poverty has been established to his satisfaction and who require such game for subsistance to himself or family.

7.—To hunt, kill or take any beaver up to the 1st of November, 1900.

8.—Any mink, otter, martin or pekan from April 1st to November 1st.

9.—Any hare from February 1st to November 1st.

10.—Any musk-rat from May 1st to January 1st.

11.—Woodcock, snipe,—from 1st February to 1st September.

12.—Partridge of any kind,—from 1st February to 15th September.

13.—Black duck, teal, wild duck of any kind, (except sheldrake and gull,)—from 1st May to 1st September.

N. B.—And at any time of the year, for the above mentionned birds, between one hour after sunset and one hour before sunrise. It is also forbidden to keep exposed, during such prohibited hours, lures, or decoys, &c.

Hunting by means of snares, springs, cages, &c.,

of any of the birds mentioned in Nos. 6, 7 and 8, is strictly prohibited.

Nevertheless in that part of the Province to the East and North of the counties of Bellechasse and Montmorency, the inhabitants may, at all seasons of the year, but only for the purpose of procuring food, shoot any of the birds mentioned in No. 8.

14.—Birds known as perchers, such as swallows, king-birds, warblers, flycatchers, woodpeckers, whippoorwills, finches, (song-sparrow, red-birds, indigo-birds, &c.,) cow-buntings, titmice, goldfinches, grives, robin, woodthrushes, &c.,) kinglets, bobolinks, grakles, grosbeaks, humming birds, cuckoos, owls, &c., except eagles, falcons, hawks, and other birds of the falconidæ, wild pigeons, king-fishers, crows, ravens, wax-wings (*récollets*), shrikes, jays, magpies, sparrow and starlings,—from 1st March to 1st September.

1.—It is forbidden to take nests or eggs of wild birds,—at any time of the year.

N. B.—Fine of $2 to $100, or imprisonment in default of payment.

No person who is not domiciled in the Province of Quebec, nor in that of Ontario can, at any time, hunt in this Province without having previously obtained a licence to that effect from the Commissioner of Crown Lands. Such permit is not transferable.

Strangers to the Province must first apply to the Commissioner of Crown Lands who, if he deems expedient, grants a game licence to the applicant on payment of a fee of from $30 to $10, according to the game sought to be hunted. This licence is valid for a whole season.

If the applicant is a member of a duly organized club in the Province the fee for the licence is only one half the regular charge.

CLOSE SEASON FOR FISHING IN THE PROVINCE OF QUEBEC.

1.—Salmon (angling),—from 15th August to 1st February.

2.—Ouananiche,—from 15th September to 1st December.

3.—Speckled trout, (*salmo fontinalis*)—from 1st October to 1st May.

4.—Large grey trout, lunge, touladi, land-locked salmon,—from 15th October to 1st December.

5.—Pickerel,—from 15th April to 15th May.

6.—Bass,—from 10th May to 1st July.

7.—Maskinongé,—from 25th May to 1st July.

8.—Whitefish,—from 15th October to 1st December.

Fine of $5 to $20, or imprisonment in default of payment.

N. B.—Angling only by hand, (with hook and line), is permitted for taking fish in the lakes and rivers under control of the Government of the Province of Quebec.

No person, who is not domiciled in the Province of Quebec, can, at any time, fish in the lakes or rivers under control of the Government of this Province, not actually under lease, without having previously obtained a permit to that effect from the Commissioner of Crown Lands. Such permit is only valid for the time, place and persons therein indicated.

www.ingramcontent.com/pod-product-compliance
Lightning Source LLC
Chambersburg PA
CBHW020910230426
43666CB00008B/1392